PRESTON

Edited by Simon Harwin

First published in Great Britain in 2003 by
YOUNG WRITERS
Remus House,
Coltsfoot Drive,
Peterborough, PE2 9JX
Telephone (01733) 890066

HB ISBN 0 75434 303 0
SB ISBN 0 75434 304 9

FOREWORD

This year, the Young Writers' The Write Stuff! competition proudly presents a showcase of the best poetic talent from over 40,000 up-and-coming writers nationwide.

Young Writers was established in 1991 and we are still successful, even in today's modern world, in promoting and encouraging the reading and writing of poetry.

The thought, effort, imagination and hard work put into each poem impressed us all, and once again, the task of selecting poems was a difficult one, but nevertheless, an enjoyable experience.

We hope you are as pleased as we are with the final selection and that you and your family continue to be entertained with *The Write Stuff! Preston* for many years to come.

CONTENTS

Jessica Dally	45
Jonathon Mclean	46
Matthew Wadsworth	46
Rachel Ramsden	47
Rachel Wearden	48
Lois Anders	48
Aaron Dawber	49
Rachael Forster	50
Oliver Yates	50
Sinéad Buckley	51
Jamie Carroll	52
Rebecca Woods	52
Gemma Melling	53
Katie Miller	54
Dominic Bowman	54
Stacey Jackson	55
Jessica Marsden	55
Beth Fraser	56
Michael Walker	56
Stephanie Forster	57
Lucy Carroll	58
Ciaran Barrek	59
Emily Hatsell	60
Natasha Fowler	60
Emma Clapham	61
Stephanie Smith	61
Peter Gartland	62
Nicola Young	63
Natalie Webb	64
Thomas Addison	64
Alexandra Gibbons	65
Stacy Bashall	66
Kelly Roddy	66
Luke Henry	67
Richard O'Sullivan	68
Kate Sedgwick	69
Lucy Jackson	70
Matthew Bradley	70

Carr Hill High School

The Poems

GHOSTS AND GHOULS

Ghosts and ghouls are very scary
Wolves in the wood are very hairy
They howl and scowl on a winter's night
And wait for the deadly morning light.
The goblins hide in the darkness cover
And wait for their once and only lover.
The ghosts fly through the hardest wall
And scare us all down the long, dark hall.
Frankenstein is large and thick
And punches like a hard stone brick.
So the ghosts and ghouls are here to stay
And the monsters try to sneak away.
The people hide, trying to leave
But will never find the door which leads
To the heavens up above and there once more
They will find the chance to live life once more.

Callum Simon (11)
All Hallows Catholic High School

A POEM FOR ANDREW

Dreams are what you're thinking,
Dreams are what you feel,
They capture every star you see
And hope they'll become real,
Because a kiss can make you happy
And a smile will fade away,
So carry your dreams with you,
Each moment,
Every day.

Bethanne Hatsell (15)
All Hallows Catholic High School

BONFIRE NIGHT

The shadowy night was as dreary as always
Although a glaring light was shining up above.
I suddenly remembered the event that was occurring
The historical event that everyone loved.

I walked a little further down the murky street
I saw some little children laughing and waving something free.
A sparkling light flickered in the darkness from what this child
was holding.
Yet a playful little thing it was it also seemed very dangerous to me.

I was still walking at this time, but shivering as well
I had caught a glimpse of something ahead, but had seemed to be
too busy.
It was spinning around with sparks flying out
As if to make me dizzy.

The final part of this mysterious event
Was far ahead in the distance from where I lurked
Although I could see this brightly coloured thing
I was told it was called a firework.

Sarah Miller (12)
All Hallows Catholic High School

PARENTS

My parents are really mad,
They drive me round the bend.
Their fashion sense is really bad,
They're worst around my friends!

They think it's fun to do homework,
They haven't got a clue.
But they'll rant and rave or go berserk,
If instead, I talk to you!

They love to boss and order me around,
They think that I'm their slave.
I think that they should lighten up
And give being a bore a wave.

Becky Fetherstone (11)
All Hallows Catholic High School

HALLOWE'EN

Boys and girls go round at night,
With a pumpkin as a light,
On the night of Hallowe'en,
Where witches and wizards can be seen,
Ghosts and ghouls
Roam round the schools,
When Dracula comes back to life,
Scream creeps round with a knife,
Zombies awake from their graves,
Sneaking round making slaves,
Goblins roam through the streets,
Knocking on doors for some sweets
Aliens come down from space
Trying to take over the human race.

Boys and girls go round at night,
With a pumpkin as a light,
They go round shouting, 'Trick or treat,'
Hoping they will get some sweets,
If they don't give them treats,
They wreak havoc down the streets,
They knock-a-door-run on your house
Sneak around the corner, quiet as a mouse,
The children go to bed at night,
Trying not to make their dreams a fright.

Katrina Murphy (13)
All Hallows Catholic High School

GREEN CHRISTMAS

Long years ago, I am sad to say,
Some things weren't merry on Christmas Day.
It was a dull and dreary scene,
'Cause all of Christmas then was green.

Our Santa dressed in olive, drab suits,
The same shade as his ugly boots
And all the elves wore dark green hats,
Green shirts, green pants and dark green cats.

There was an elf among the crew
Who planted stuff that grew and grew.
A sort of legend, he'd become,
He had red hair and one green thumb.

Old Santa liked this elf called Ned
He called him in one day and said,
'It would be nice if we'd display
A special plant on Christmas Day.'

Hollie Bretherton (13)
All Hallows Catholic High School

THE FISHERMAN

The fisherman was a silent man,
He was clever and his name was Dan,
Dan could catch a lot of fish with his special rod,
He could catch all sorts including cod.

He went to the river every day,
Whether it be rainy and windy or sunny in May,
Blue ones, green ones, are all he's caught,
Use dead bait is what he was taught.

He sat on the bank in his chair,
Catching something that's really rare,
He sat there all day and sometimes went to sleep,
With all that he's caught in a great big heap.

Then Dan went home, back to his house,
So late that everywhere was as quiet as a mouse,
He wandered, he walked down the empty streets,
Only to hear the sound of his heartbeat.

Jordan Chowdhury (14)
All Hallows Catholic High School

SEASONS

Winter is cold over here,
We have to wrap up in our warm gear.
Winter is near when there is frost,
I wonder how much Christmas must cost?

Spring is great over here,
We have to get out all the Easter gear.
Spring brings up a lot of new things,
It's really great what spring brings.

Summer is warm over here,
We have to get out our holiday gear.
Summer heat gives us a tan,
It makes us need to use a fan.

Autumn is great over here,
We have to get out our cosy gear.
Autumn is great while it lasts, then
Winter is ready to begin again.

Daniel Bunce (11)
All Hallows Catholic High School

MY DOG

My dog is an English bull terrier
And has a very long nose
He struts about around the place
And leaves amazed faces wherever he goes.

His name is Duke,
But he doesn't match his name,
He barks and barks and wags his tail,
But he can be very tame.

I must end this poem
Saying one more thing
And it is, that even though Duke looks fierce
He's really very soft!

Sophie McNabb (11)
All Hallows Catholic High School

ANIMALS POEM

I like animals
They're as cool as can be,
I love animals
And they like me.

Dogs, cats and rabbits,
Hamsters, fish and mice,
Whatever animal, big or small,
I think they're rather nice.

Horses are quite cute,
But dogs are simply the best,
All animals are really cool,
But spiders are just a pest.

Kate Lambert (11)
All Hallows Catholic High School

THE MAN ON THE BENCH

I walk past him every day
He smiles at me
And I always say,
'Why do you sit there every day?'
He replies,
'It makes me happy in every way.'

I look again and still he is there
I wonder why he doesn't care
That people think he is such a freak
Sitting there week after week.

Day after day people walk past
They see him and then walk fast
But I don't care what he chooses to do
And so I join him and sit down too.

Penelope Holmes (13)
All Hallows Catholic High School

MY FRIENDS

My friend Gemma is really cool.
My friend Becky likes to act the fool.
My friend Katrina's great at art.
My friend Alicia well she's always smart.
My friend Laura's really, really fun.
My friend Serena is as bright as the sun.
My friend Vicky is bright and sunny.
My friend Lucy's really funny.
My friend Sam, she's great at Irish dancing.
My friend Nicole's sporty, good at prancing.
As you can see my friends are great,
Why don't you just tell a mate!

Ruth Kaye (13)
All Hallows Catholic High School

MY FAMILY

First of all there is my dad,
At heart he's really still a lad,
Watches telly,
Eats ice cream and jelly
And life in general, he's just mad.

Next in line is my mum,
Who isn't much taller than a crumb,
She is so small,
That she could crawl,
Inside anyone's tum.

Then came along my sister Jenny,
Who will spend anything, a pound or a penny,
She loves to shop,
But won't touch a mop,
My dear sister Jenny.

Finally my brother Tom,
I think that he could well be from
A different world
And he was hurled
Inside the tum of my mom.

Danny Hoyle (12)
All Hallows Catholic High School

MY FRIENDS

My friends are always there for me,
I know I'm not alone
Even when I close my eyes,
I always know they're there.

I think that they're the greatest
I know they will help me up
If I fall down.

Small, tall, fat or thin,
Who cares what they look like,
Because they're always there for me.

My friends, my friends,
They're the greatest,
Because they're my friends.

Samantha Parr (13)
All Hallows Catholic High School

THE LILYWHITES

Down Sir Tom Finney Way
Oh my, what a sight
Deepdale the home of football
Was shining bright.

The football museum
In all of its glory
Each exhibit tells a story.

Go through the turnstiles
Enter the ground
Refreshments and programmes
Can be found.

This is Deepdale where Preston play
Cresswell scores and Tepi saves
Into my seat in the Kelly stand
We start to sing along with the band.

The whistle blows, we start to play
Fuller scores, we're on our way
Ninety minutes of talent and skill
Win promotion? Of course we will!

Thomas Campbell (11)
All Hallows Catholic High School

SEASONS, DAY AND NIGHT

There is no sound,
There is no light,
Apart from the street lamps
Shining bright.

The sun is shining
In the sky
Above the clouds
Way up high.

Leaves are falling,
The trees are bare,
The squirrels are sleeping
Way up there.

The snow is falling,
Oh, it's cold,
Look at the snowmen
Who never grow old.

Laura Burke (13)
All Hallows Catholic High School

EGYPT

Along the edge of the River Nile,
That stretches far, for miles and miles.
A boat sails past a crocodile,
That's resting by the River Nile.
While in the sand a scorpion crawls
And peasants make bricks for the palace walls,
The statues stand up so straight and tall,
But the flies in the air buzz about so small.

Matthew Keefe (12)
All Hallows Catholic High School

My Friend Billy

My friend Billy
Is as silly as a dog.
He's got legs like a rabbit
And arms like a frog.

His eyebrows are so bushy
And his hair's as black as coal.
His eyes are small and squinty,
Just like his pet mouse, Paul.

He plays football for our team
And his kick's as hard as rock.
He always wins a tackle
With an elbow or a knock.

He thinks he is the best
And can't help acting silly.
He behaves just like a clown,
That's my friend Billy!

Ryan Alty (12)
All Hallows Catholic High School

United

United are the best
Better than all the rest
With the likes of Nistelrooy, Giggs and Scholes
Always scoring the goals
With a brilliant midfield
And the defence like a shield
United are the best
Better than all the rest.

Jonathan Curry (13)
All Hallows Catholic High School

DEAR GRANDAD

I know you're looking down
Looking down to see
Everything that's happening
Happening to me.

Everything I do right
Everything I do wrong
I know you're always there
Helping me to be strong.

My brother and my sister
My cousins and my aunts
My uncles and my mum and dad
We all had a chance

To know you and to love
Until the day we part
It's not the end yet though
It's only just the start

Of a new life for all of us
But the memory will never leave
Of you my dear grandad
Give you happiness, please.

Laura Grundy (13)
All Hallows Catholic High School

LIVING IN MY MEMORY

I think of you sitting in your chair
Only to remember that you're not there
And it all comes back to me
Like a film I went to see.

That now you're gone, that now you're dead,
That you only live inside my head.
But in a way you're here with me
Living in my memory.

Lauren Dedman (13)
All Hallows Catholic High School

THE DARK

We are in a dark room.
Isolation: a telescope and a window.
The stars. We look at the dark sky.
'How would you describe yourself?'
'A geographer, a scientist, a wonderer?'
'An artist?'
'Yes, I work on the mysterious things you see in the newspaper,
Black holes, space phenomenon.'
We must fly.
The moon, the moon is in our wake.
We approach the city,
Its light glinting, like a giant circuit board,
Its roads, its life.
Humanity believes we have escaped the dark.
The lights of the city, we make, shield us from the dark.
This is a lie.
We cannot escape the dark.
People never leave the house, the office, the car,
They never know the dark, but it is there nonetheless.

The stars,
The city lights,
The dark,
We cannot escape the dark . . .

Richard Bowman (14)
All Hallows Catholic High School

THE COLOURFUL LEAVES

I walked down a country lane
In my coat and boots
I saw red, yellow, brown leaves
Drifting in the wind.

The clouds were grey and fluffy
On a winter's eve
It will not be the same again
Until I feel a summer breeze.

My nose feels a tickle so I sneeze
I look up and see the bare trees
On the floor are colourful leaves
Soft and silky
Leaves in the sky, lovely and dry.

Luke Davis (13)
All Hallows Catholic High School

WINTER

Winter is brutally cold
Its power has been foretold.
Winter will bite the toes from your feet
Winter will make all warmth fleet,
Killing it, the warmth soon dies
For a long time the winter will thrive.
But then the sun will become stronger
The winter lives not for much longer.
Winter dissolves - a washed-up has-been
The sunlight crushes the cold with its beam
Winter is silenced once more
But he'll be back, to rule once more.

James McEwan (11)
All Hallows Catholic High School

Is It . . . ?

As calm as the ocean,
As rough as the sea?

As small as today,
As big as tomorrow?

As warm as winter.
As icy as spring?

As bright as the night,
As dark as the stars?

As loud as a whisper,
As quiet as a scream?

To my ears
It's poetry.

Jessica Clemo (13)
All Hallows Catholic High School

Winter Wind

W inter is here, the wind is there.
I n the trees and running and leaping through the air.
N ear the fruitless, leafless apple tree that stands on the hill
T he wind is cold, even gives winter a chill.
E very time the wind and winter mix then comes,
R oof tiles and frost-bitten trees creak and hum.

W hoosh, swish all around,
I n the yard like a hound
N ever to be ignored
D emonstrating its strength to our Lord.

Sophie Ellis (11)
All Hallows Catholic High School

SOMETHING IS HAPPENING!

Something is going to happen, so go and tell a friend,
It's going to happen very soon and never, ever end.
You don't know what is happening, so you've got to be aware,
When darkness comes, you're all alone, you're going to get a scare.
The time is coming, it's nearly night,
As you know you're going to get a fright.
This thing is big, it's mean and scary,
It's gruesome, bad and really hairy.
It has big feet and massive claws,
This thing is going, so you've gotta go.
I don't want to be really mean,
So I'll give you a clue, it's nearly
Hallowe'en!

Jessica Johnson (12)
All Hallows Catholic High School

MY SIS, SAMANTHA

My sister Samantha is cute although . . .
She can be a pain . . . when she wants to
She can mess up her room . . . when she wants to
She'll go to bed late . . . when she wants to
She draws on my homework . . . when she wants to
She bites me and hits me . . . when she wants to
She can be very lazy . . . when she wants to be
She can be an attention seeker . . . when she wants to be
She can whine all the time . . . when she wants to
She can eat all her tea . . . when she wants to
She can scream and shout very loudly . . . when she wants to
She can wear impractical clothes . . . when she wants to
But I tell you what . . . it's not very often.

Gemma Wilkinson (13)
All Hallows Catholic High School

BUT...

We live on a beautiful planet,
But we destroy it.
So much nature,
But we build on it.
So much food,
But people starve.
We celebrate our lives,
But we take them from each other.
There is birth and life,
But pain and death.
There are happy people,
But others who are sad.
We are all brothers and sisters,
But there is no peace.
There is destruction all around,
But we do nothing about it.
There are always 'buts' in our lives,
But we dream of a life without any.

Phillip Purcell (13)
All Hallows Catholic High School

THE SUN

The sun is like a golden ball,
Sitting on my garden wall.
It comes up early in the morning,
Then at night it goes down yawning.
Every day I sit and stare,
To see if it moves from here to there.
Then each night I go to bed,
I look out of the window, but the moon's there instead.

Amy Fox (13)
All Hallows Catholic High School

MY DAY!

My alarm clock awakes me at 7 o'clock,
I look for my clothes, oh where is that sock?

My mum shouts me down that breakfast is ready,
My brother is halfway through his already.

I'm off to the bus stop for quarter-past eight,
I'll have to hurry, I don't want to be late.

When I arrive at school the bell is ringing,
The first lesson is music, I think we'll be singing.

The morning goes slow, I can't wait for my break,
I've forgotten my homework . . . oh big mistake!

My favourite lesson is tech, that's all afternoon,
My journey home will be happening soon.

When I get home I can text my mate,
To see if her day has been just as great.

I want to go out, but Mum says homework comes first,
The way she shouts, I sometimes think she will burst.

I'm starving now, I fancy a snack,
But Mum says, 'No, put that back!'

It's sausage for dinner, that I don't like,
I just want to go out and play on my bike.

But the dark nights are coming and I've no lights,
So I'll just stay in and watch TV, it's EastEnders tonight.

I make myself a bite of supper
And a cup of tea, I do love a cuppa.

It's 10 o'clock now and time for my bed,
I can stay up late tomorrow, my mum said.

I close my eyes and start to dream,
Thinking about tomorrow's similar scene.

Amy Louise Ford (12)
All Hallows Catholic High School

THE APPLE TREE!

It was under this very apple tree
When I kicked my first football,
I wasn't very good
But I enjoyed it.

It was under this very apple tree
That I ate my first worm,
I liked the taste
But I was only a baby.

It was under this very apple tree
I spoke my first words,
They were Santa Claus
Santa must be thrilled.

It was under this very apple tree,
I got my first toy car,
I pushed it about
The driver's head fell off.

It was under this very apple tree
When I first played on a Game Boy,
The game was Bugs Bunny
It was terrific fun!

James Barbuto (11)
All Hallows Catholic High School

RULE THE SCHOOL

I dreamt that I'd taken over the school,
Made all the teachers wear school uniform,
Kicked the head teacher out for changing the rules,
Got the pupils to give the teachers a good lesson,
Went to the staffroom, changed all the reports,
Gave the teachers a detention to clean all 102 doors,
Went to the shops and bought bags of sweets,
Shared them with the pupils before the teachers got to eat,
Started to hailstone and chuck it down with rain,
Made the teachers stand outside and cry out with pain,
Ten minutes before home time,
Let the pupils out early before they got homework,
Made the teachers stay in,
Made them clean all the rooms with rubbish in the bin,
10pm let them go.

Gillian Henry (13)
All Hallows Catholic High School

HELP ME!

A distant scream is all I hear
I would help - if I was near
If I was rich I'd give money away -
But I am not, so I won't pay
My feet are tired, my eyes begin to drop,
I fall asleep, from the bottom to the top.
I hear a noise, I lie awake in bed,
Terrorising thoughts, coursing through my head
My door creaks open, I see a knife,
I clutch my quilt, fear for my life
I let out a cry of fright, a little plea,
I just wish somebody would help me.

Heather Naylor (13)
All Hallows Catholic High School

MY CAT

I love my cat,
She's terribly fat.
She spends all day,
Sleeping away.

But at night it is a different tale,
She hunts the wildlife without fail.
Though they seem to get away,
She chases them every day.

But I hope one day she will see,
Hunting creatures is not to be.
Perhaps she will decide to stay
And let them live another day.

Antonia Parry (11)
All Hallows Catholic High School

LIVERPOOL FC

Liverpool are good and great
Police always stand at the gates
They always win
And they always score
That makes teams always bored
Owen is the very best
Heskey has a hairy chest
Gerrard is a great ball player
Murphy is a good goal scorer
Hamman is a good explorer
And Diouf is a brilliant ignorer
Riise is very plain, when he comes on
It starts to rain.

Tyler Bennett (13)
All Hallows Catholic High School

WHEN MY TOILET STARTS TO GRUNT

When my toilet starts to grunt
It always startles me
It grunts when I'm in the toilet
Trying to have a wee.

When my toilet starts to grunt
Beware it doesn't frighten you
For it grunts when you are sitting down
Trying to have a poo.

As I try and do my business
Behind an overgrown bush
From the open bathroom window
I hear the grunting toilet flush.

And as my mum and dad discussed
What to do with the angry bog
I was out behind the bush
Doing my business in thick fog.

Nor I dare to set foot in there
For a long, long time to come
But it's cold out here behind the bush
But it's worth the freezing bum.

And as the plumber came round next morning
He tutted as he looked
But it's worth the noise coming from upstairs
To shut the grunting rust bucket up.

At last I can poo and wee again
The toilet is free for all
'No more grunting from there, no way,'
I very merrily called.

And as the zip shuts the hood
Of the rusty, angry metal lump
And now the peace is extremely good
As I go for my morning dump.

Joe Minniss (13)
All Hallows Catholic High School

MRS BRIGHT?

Mrs Bright had a fright,
In the middle of the night.
Saw a ghost eating toast,
Half-way up the lamp-post.
So she ran out of the house,
Followed by a great big mouse.
Off she ran, it was no fun,
To be out at night with an empty tum.
Off she went to the late night shop,
To buy a big fat juicy chop.
She looked here, she looked there,
She could not find one anywhere.
She asked the staff and they just laughed,
They said, 'No, just go.'
When she went back home, she saw no ghosts,
To be seen on the lamp-posts.
She found some chops after all that,
To feed her and her big fat cat.
After that she watched television,
She had to wear glasses for her poor vision.
When her programme had ended,
She went to bed with her cat Ned.

Charmaine Vas (11)
All Hallows Catholic High School

JUST A CHANCE...

Sitting on the street with nowhere to go,
Life's getting me down, it's making me low.
People walk past - a smug look on their face,
Looking at me like I'm a waste of space.

But I'm better than that, for I wouldn't ignore you,
A fellow human being - I'm not below you.
I own nothing, have nothing to wear,
But at least I have a heart and at least I care.

Living on the street, no job, all alone,
Yet you're so comfy sat in your home.
Watching your telly, all warm by the fire,
No thoughts of me when it's cold and dire.

To escape from this madness I just need a chance
So stop walking past and cast me a glance.
You think it's only my sadness keeping me here,
But your views of me are so insincere.

When you have plenty, I go without,
What's left in this world for me - a so-called down and out?
I don't want your sympathy or charity,
Just give me a chance to show what I can be.

People judge me before they know
The hardship I have seen or love I have to show.
So next time you see me, don't just walk past,
All I want is a chance to show I can last.

Sarah McDonnell (14)
All Hallows Catholic High School

BUFFY TIN

My friend is very scruffy,
She looks just like a bin,
Her first name is Buffy,
Her second name is Tin.

My friend is so disorganised,
She always rings me up,
I never get surprised,
When she hasn't got her book.

At school she's really mean,
She thinks she's number one!
She always causes a scene
And thinks that this is fun!

Her clothes are very tatty,
She looks just like a tramp,
Her hair is very scratty
And it's always damp.

She's got strong feelings,
About love and hate,
But she doesn't know the meaning
Of being a good mate.

Her head's the size of a ball,
Her brain's the size of a pea,
She's not my friend at all,
She's my worst enemy!

Louise Bamber (13)
All Hallows Catholic High School

THE PIG'S MANNERS

This pig's manners are quite appalling
You really don't want to know,
He scoffs his food as fast as he can
It's really quite a show.

This pig's manners are quite appalling
He rolls around in mud
And seriously, quite honestly
He'd pick his nose if he could.

This pig's manners are quite appalling
So stay away if you please
Oh no, watch out and run away
This pig's about to *sneeze!*

Melissa Moore (11)
All Hallows Catholic High School

31ST OF OCTOBER

Hallowe'en is a creepy time,
A time for trick or treating.
Ghosts and ghouls come out at night,
On the 31st of October.

Hallowe'en is a scary time,
A time for crazy pumpkin faces.
Vampires come out and suck your blood
On the 31st of October.

Hallowe'en is a wicked time,
A time to scare your mum.
You put a spider in her bed
On the 31st of October.

Tanyel Goren (12)
All Hallows Catholic High School

ALL AROUND

Look at the ground,
What do you see?
A blade of grass,
Or an earthworm for me?

Look at the sky,
What do you see?
A big, fluffy cloud,
Or the sun maybe?

When I look around,
I see what God made,
A beautiful world,
Which will never ever fade.

Tom Swayne (13)
All Hallows Catholic High School

I AM A TREE

I am a tree
That stands here still,
I have a friend
His name is Dill.

I sit on my own
All night and day,
I've been sitting here
Since last May.

I'm nearly an adult
But I still need to grow,
I like watching
The big moon glow.

Emma Burke (11)
All Hallows Catholic High School

HAVE YOU EVER WONDERED WHY?

Have you ever wondered why
Water's wet and land is dry?
Maybe cos water didn't reach
For example, the sunny beach.

Have you ever wondered why
Humans walk and birds can fly?
Maybe cos the reason is why,
The ground is low and the sky is high.

Have you ever wondered why
Adults laugh and babies cry?
Maybe cos adults stay happy,
While their babies have a dirty nappy.

Have you ever wondered why
What's the difference between a bee and a fly?
Maybe cos a bee will buzz,
Whilst a fly on your meal will make a fuss.

Have you ever wondered why
This poem will always rhyme?
But not for long anymore,
Cos I've run out of many different thoughts.

Liz Skingsley (11)
All Hallows Catholic High School

AUTUMN

Underfoot the leaves are crunching,
In the woods the squirrels are munching.
The rabbits come out to play
The birds all fly away.
The leaves are brown
And tumble down,
On a windy day.

When autumn comes, the flowers all die,
When the sun is out, it's low in the sky.
The nights are long, the days are cooler,
Winter is just around the corner.

Andrew Astley (13)
All Hallows Catholic High School

HALLOWE'EN NIGHT

Come out of your house,
Walk down the street,
Getting ready to play,
Trick or treat.
Everyone's dressed,
In black and white,
Ready to scare,
The October night.
After you've played,
The practical joke,
You turn round to see,
The faint, black smoke.
See the fireworks,
Round about,
Hear all the children,
Scream and shout.
As you walk,
Down the street,
All dressed up,
Counting your sweets.
It's getting late,
Time for bed,
The children go,
To home, I head.

Georgie Fox (12)
All Hallows Catholic High School

NOTHING

She thought she heard a footstep on the landing
'Nothing,' she said to herself.
'There's nothing there.'
She then thought she heard a cough in the lounge.
'Nothing,' she said to herself again
'Nothing at all.'
But she daren't get out of her seat
Just in case nothing was there
After staying quiet in her seat
She asked herself if there was anything there?
Her answer was nothing, because there was nothing there -
Again!

Rebecca Swarbrick (11)
All Hallows Catholic High School

FLU

I'm lying in bed I feel quite cranky.
I sneezed before my tissue was manky.
I'm hot and sticky and a little bit sweaty,
I want to go to school but my mum won't let me.
The doc's been called, he's coming quite soon,
He's got to see me in my sick room.
I shout my mum but she's fed up,
Of running around like a demented pup.
The doctor's here he gives me a pill,
It's not working I feel even more ill.
Don't come near me you could get it too.
Do you know what I've got, it's the *flu!*

Ryan Ingram (12)
All Hallows Catholic High School

A Short Cut To Lose Weight!

Eye of cat,
Wing of bat,
Foot of dog,
Guts of frog.

Mix it up,
Make it sticky,
This spell isn't very tricky.

A few more things to add to the pot,
Blood, bones, the puss of a spot.

Cook it well,
It's a slimming dinner
After eating this, you'll be much thinner.

Hayley Doel (11)
All Hallows Catholic High School

A Smile!

A smile is a funny thing,
But look at all the joy it brings.

It's just like an upside-down frown,
But it never makes people feel down.

A smile is something all so mellow,
It won't make anyone feel they're turning yellow.

A smile is not at all bad,
It will never make people sad.

A smile is the opposite of mean,
It will never make you turn green.

Fianna Hornby (11)
All Hallows Catholic High School

TIME

The past holds power upon us all,
The future holds mysterious, yet untold,
Access to these we are denied,
Although many of us have tried.

Time machines and other things,
Made for emperors and kings,
Over time to live forever,
Yet, power over time will be ours never.

Time is a stage, our entrances we know,
Our exits come upon us suddenly, but we still have to go,
Nothing can be changed, nothing at all,
We cannot direct and we do not give the calls.

Time; beginning, middle and end,
Time to keep and time to spend,
Time to wait for what's to come
And time to finish, what's begun.

Jennifer McMichael (15)
All Hallows Catholic High School

TRICK OR TREAT

Children out in costumes
Yelling, 'Trick or treat.'
Coming back with rotting teeth
Because of all the sweets.

Some are so generous
Giving lots of sweets
Others though, they just yell,
'Get lost you'll get no treats.'

Julia Wheatley (11)
All Hallows Catholic High School

SHEER DELIGHT!

I'm going to describe
Something close to my heart
And here it is, right from the start.

It comes as a flake,
It comes as a cake,
It's bought as a bar,
Between four, it won't go far.

You can drink it,
You can eat it
And you really . . .
Can't beat it.

It's dark, it's white
It's creamy and light
It's good in the day
But yummy at night.

Hannah Devaney (12)
All Hallows Catholic High School

BONFIRE NIGHT

On a black night the noises go,
The smell of the toffees flow,
Up the fireworks go
And down comes Guy,
While the colours flash in your eye,
The fire spits out the heat,
But the mud eats your feet,
The stars twinkle,
The leaves of the fire grow
While we watch and glow.

Nicola McAvoy (13)
All Hallows Catholic High School

MY BED

When I'm in my bed,
All the thoughts in my head,
Can go wandering far and wide.

Snuggled up all cosy,
My cheeks red and rosy
I prefer it to being outside.

I don't get hot
And cold I'm not
And my hands are toasty warm (makes a change!)

Now in my dreams,
Everything, it seems,
Can be OK in a flash!

To wrap up this rhyme,
I don't have much time,
I love my bed to pieces!

Jessica Robertson (13)
All Hallows Catholic High School

FISH

Fish swim around in tanks
And yesterday one of my fish sank.
Around the tank they swim,
The glass makes them look slim.

In a bowl, in a pond,
In the sea they all belong.
In the sea it's really dark,
So fish, beware of the shark.

Jenny Delaney (11)
All Hallows Catholic High School

MY BROTHER

He is 21 years old and still lives with us
He always catches the Preston bus.
He goes out on a Saturday night
And always sees a great big fight.
When he watches football,
He shouts when it's a goal.
Whenever he sees my dog,
He says, 'It looks like a frog.'
Whenever he goes hunting
I always try and thump him
And say, 'It's cruel to shoot
'Cause all they do is hoot.'
He argues with my mother
After all, he is my brother.

Damian Baines (12)
All Hallows Catholic High School

HAPPY DAYS

The sea was lapping against the sand
I lay down amongst the sand
The boats were bobbing upon the waves
They were loyal, almost slaves
To the sea, the mighty sea,
Sparkling so beautifully.
The wind was calm,
The people gay,
The sun shone down on where I lay
Then the sun, its golden rays
Hid behind the clouds so grey
In so many different ways
It made me think of happy days.

Lydia Schofield (11)
All Hallows Catholic High School

AWAKENING

In the distance a high-pitched bell summons me into day.
The sound grows louder and louder, until wide awake
Shaken from my slumber, the alarm clock,
Suddenly silenced by my outstretched hand.

Wanting to curl up and disappear into sleep once more,
The day is too bright to face,
Duty calls, time for school.
So reluctantly, I force myself to struggle
from the warmth of my blankets.

The day begins to envelop me,
Filling my head with sights and sounds.
Frantic movements, a tirade of thoughts and speech.
This life is so frantic, busy, deafening,
More than I can bear sometimes.

The day hurtles on
Spinning me around and around in its rush.
No time to slow down
No time to feel the moment
No time to relax
Impossible to switch off.

Can I make sense of it all?
Where will it end?
Will I be able to unscramble the chaos around me?
Keep going, that's all I can do,
Soon I will be finding my way home.
Soon I will find some peace.

At last the day ends, the safety and silence of sleep beckons.
Not so easy to escape the madness of the day.
I long to sleep, to forget, to curl up and lose myself
in drowsiness and slumber.
Until the distant bell calls me once again
Back to the explosion of the day.

Francesca Jackson (14)
All Hallows Catholic High School

FOUR SEASONS

Cups of sunshine
spread along the grass
buds spring open
showing beauty to all that pass.

Frogs in the lily pond
birds in the trees
ducklings paddling along
in the mid-summer breeze.

The bright sun dulls
and the leaves fall to the ground
leaving nature's many colours
strewn all around.

The woodlands turn brown and bare
until the white snow and the frost leaves its trail
and winter finally defeats the stream
to freeze the calm, still waters.

That's the four season story.

Elizabeth Moore (11)
All Hallows Catholic High School

JEALOUS

Jealousy running wild
As they watch the wealthy child,
Bikes, toys, clothes and looks
All they want is a few books.
The boy has got it all,
They'd be happy to see a mall!
These poor children had nothing to name
Except hunger and pain.

Every day slowly goes by
As they hope for a friend to say, 'Hi.'
They get called for how they look,
To others they're just a pile of muck.
Some day they will be heard
And hopefully get what they deserve.
Till that day they will remain the 'freaks'
But soon they will call them back, 'Geeks!'

Colette Atkinson (13)
All Hallows Catholic High School

WINNIE THE POOH AND FRIENDS

Piglet is so cuddly
Unlike Rabbit who is ugly
Eeyore is hardly ever happy
'Cause he is a grumpy chappy
You can't forget Kanga and little Roo
Who are good friends of Winnie the Pooh
As Christopher Robin grows bigger
He likes to bounce around with Tigger
They all live in the Hundred Acre Wood
You can only go there if you're good.

Kelsey Davenport (12)
All Hallows Catholic High School

MY LIFE POEM

When I was one I learned to walk
When I was two I learned to talk

When I was three I tried school
When I was four I went to school

When I was five I made some new friends
When I was six I learned my table times ten

When I was seven I started reading
When I was eight I started singing

When I was nine I saw my first bat
When I was ten I had my SATs

When I was eleven I went into first year
Now that I'm twelve I look back over the years
And say, 'That's my life.'

Edel Bean (12)
All Hallows Catholic High School

CHOCOLATE

Mars bars, Crunchies, Dairy Milk,
Rolos, Buttons, Nestlé Silk,
Echoes, Wispas and a Twix
I've got to have my chocolate fix.
Chocolate puddings, cookies as well
I just love that chocolate smell.
Chocolate for breakfast, dinner and tea
Get that chocolate inside me.

Clare Shepherd (11)
All Hallows Catholic High School

WHY DOES TOAST ALWAYS LAND BUTTER-SIDE DOWN?

Why does toast always land butter-side down?
It makes me want to frown,
I pick it up with hair and fluff
And other bits of horrible stuff.
Butter gets everywhere,
But the worst bit . . .
It gets in my hair,
And when I've just washed it too
And then I say, 'Now I'm through.'
I put it down the toilet and flush,
Man it's been a heck of a rush.
I hear my mum coming down the stairs,
My eyes blow up and my nose . . . it flares.
I run, run, run as fast as I can,
The force of my speed, it makes the door slam.
Plates are smashing,
Knives are clashing,
My mum's coming down the hall
And I trip up and bounce off the wall.
My mum opens the door,
It opens more and more,
But all she said that moment, right then,
'Toast land butter-side down again?'

Kathryn Heatley (11)
All Hallows Catholic High School

THE WEEKEND!

The weekend starts on Friday afternoon,
Hear the school bell ring, I'm over the moon,
End of the day I have to walk home,
Weekend's coming, I'm glad I'm not alone,
End of Friday, start of new,

Early Saturday morning let's go to the zoo,
Katie my friend stays over for tea,
Evening time comes, let's go to the sea,
Night-time falls, I have to go to bed,
Dreaming about the full week ahead.

Jessica Westney (12)
All Hallows Catholic High School

PETS NEXT DOOR

I shut the door and go out to play
As I heard the next-door neighbour's horse go, 'neigh!'

I play on the swing, going up and down
I looked over at the Highland cow which gave me a frown.

I hop on my bike, ready to ride
As I see the dog jump over our side.

I run to my mum who's doing the tea
She got so angry, she went mad at me.

She said, 'Where's that man? I need words with him.'
Just as the dog jumped back in.

It was dark and I was trying to sleep,
Then I heard 'Baaa!' it was his sheep.

My dad got angry and I got mad
I heard my dad sigh, 'That man is bad.'

The very next day I heard no more
As I saw the animals asleep on the floor.

I was so happy, I had nothing to say
Because I was so thankful for that very day.

Heather Cookson (12)
All Hallows Catholic High School

MY WEEKEND POEM

It's Friday the school bell rings,
Happiness runs through my veins.
School is finished for the weekend,
Still got too much school work to do
So not all my time is free.
Go home, listen to music and watch TV, relaxing.
Wish I had more free time to hang around with my mates
And have less homework
At least I get to stay up late.
My mum, neighbours and I are upset
About a friend because he had a heart attack,
So it has not been a very happy weekend.
My brother got a weekend job; my mum and dad
Are happier and I think it is great because he is
Out of my way for the day.

Stefano Di Franco (12)
All Hallows Catholic High School

DREAMS

Some dreams are good
And some are bad,
A few of them can make me sad,
When I dream that I can fly,
Very high into the sky,
The clouds are white and fluffy too,
Sometimes I always dream of you,
I may dream of devils and fire,
Where the flames get higher and higher
And when my dream is over and one,
My heart starts pounding like a drum.

Laura Martland (12)
All Hallows Catholic High School

CAMPING

The morning is bright,
But it was stormy last night.
As I lay down in my bed,
The night filled me with dread.
The wind started rustling through the trees,
It's alright, it is only a breeze.
The wind got stronger I could feel it through the tent,
It was bending and swaying on the side it leant.
As I thought it was over,
The rain started tapping,
Then the thunder was clapping,
I thought the tent was going to fly,
Right into the sky.
Will I survive
Or ever get out alive?

Elizabeth House (11)
All Hallows Catholic High School

WHY?

Why cry
When we can laugh?
Why frown
When we can smile?
Why hate
When we can love?
Why should people be hungry
When there's enough for us all to eat?
Why fight
When we can all live in peace?

Why?

Jonathon Pill (12)
All Hallows Catholic High School

SMELLS

There's a smell of burnt toast,
When I leave for school,
I close the door because
It's enough to make you drool.

I smell freshly cut grass,
As I walk down the street,
It was cut only last night,
So the smell is still sweet.

As I enter the building
And smell the musty scent,
I have smelt it so many times,
It's proof of the time at school I've spent.

When dinner time comes,
I smell those chips,
It wafts up my nose
As they touch my lips.

When I leave school,
I smell the crave,
Chocolate Swiss rolls,
Only 15p at Kwik Save.

I begin my journey home,
I need to find a solution,
To all those whining babies,
Then my nose gets a whiff of car pollution.

As I enter my house,
There's a stuffy smell,
I turn the alarm off
And open some windows as well.

I've completed my day of all things smelly,
So sit down, feet up and switch on the telly.

Jennifer Rossall (12)
All Hallows Catholic High School

BLACKPOOL

If you prefer a quiet visit to the beach,
Hearing the seagulls screech,
Building castles, swimming in the sea,
The waves and the sand,
Oh what fun!

Oh, then again there's the Pepsi Max,
Hear people scream and have a laugh,
Swaying backwards,
Swaying fro,
Swaying as fast as you can go.

If you don't like heights,
Then you wouldn't want to be
Anywhere near
Blackpool Tower.

Yes, Blackpool is the place to be
Come with me and you shall see
Why I chose
Blackpool!

Jessica Dally (11)
All Hallows Catholic High School

HOMEWORK

Homework, homework is so bad
Homework can drive you really mad,
You get it nearly every day
So you can't go out and play, play, play.

I get really bored doing it all
Sometimes I feel like I'm going to fall,
I get too much, but I don't complain
Because my friend is doing the same.

It takes up all of the night
Therefore I have to sit in the light,
My mum comes in, I'm finally done
So now I go out and have some fun.

I go back to school and hand it in
And I hope the teacher doesn't throw it in the bin,
I get it back the next day
And I have got a brilliant 'A'.

So after all my brilliant work
I can now go home and smirk, smirk, smirk.

Jonathon Mclean (12)
All Hallows Catholic High School

WINTER

Winter is the coldest time of the year,
Snow falls from the sky (and it lands near).
Throwing snowballs at everyone,
Winter, winter it's lots of fun.

Wintertime sledding down the icy hill,
But wrap up warm and watch out for the chill.
Building snowmen with their carrot nose,
The snow freezes children's fingers and toes.

Winter is the best season of all,
With its own special winter fall.
When Christmas time comes near,
At 24th December men will be drinking beer.

Matthew Wadsworth (11)
All Hallows Catholic High School

WANNA BE

In the future I can see,
What I'm gonna be.
A pop idol to sing all night
And I will shine in the light.

A hippy chick that's blind to see,
That's what I wanna be.
Hit the music, count to three,
Fame and fortune here to see.

Strike the music, hear the sound,
Thousands of people gather round.
Supermodel I will be,
Everyone will look at me.
The catwalk's where I wanna be.

People cheer and people scream,
Oh no, is this just a dream?
Is this a dream or am I awake?
A thousand number 1s I'll make.

I hear a sound, the alarm bell goes,
Where I've been, no one knows.
The fame and fortune was so great,
But now it's over, I have to *wait*.

Rachel Ramsden (12)
All Hallows Catholic High School

MY DAD IS AN ELVIS FAN

My dad is an Elvis fan,
He likes the King of Rock,
He thinks the world of the greatest man,
But not the fans that mock.

Elvis rules the world of pop,
No one to claim his crown,
In death he has no need to stop,
No one can bring him down.

Gareth Gates did Suspicious Minds,
What an awful try,
He wants to be Elvis in his life,
But Elvis fans need not cry.

There is no one to claim the crown,
So greatly it is worn,
But people like Gareth Gates,
Will never pull the crowds.

Rachel Wearden (12)
All Hallows Catholic High School

CANDYFLOSS HEAD

I know a guy his name is Ted
he was born with a candyfloss head.
In the mornin' when he gets out of bed
he can't but notice his big, pink head.
It's big and pink and tastes of sugar
his dad said, 'You look like your mother.'

It glows in the dark and it is quite bright
and children think he's a traffic light!
His hair is like a pink bush
but it is very hard to brush.

He decided to give it a wash
but oh no, it turned to mush.
'What will I do? Look at my hair!'
But then he dyed it blond
and now it's fair!

Lois Anders (11)
All Hallows Catholic High School

MY FOUR-LEGGED FRIENDS

Bichon Frise's, that's what they are,
With boundless energy, they can run quite far.
They leap and run just like they're crazy,
My beautiful puppies Skye and Daisy.
When morning comes, from their beds they creep,
All white and fluffy, just like sheep.

They jump on my bed and want to play,
So pleased to see another day.
Getting dressed for me is quite a feat,
They steal my socks and bite my feet.
When I leave for school I feel quite bad,
My lovely puppies look so sad.

My day's full of thoughts of Skye and Daisy,
Although they'll be sleeping, they are quite lazy.
When I come home they're so pleased to meet me,
Wagging their tails as they run to greet me.
I know if my puppies could talk,
They would say, 'Aaron, it's time for a walk.'

So down to the field we go to play
And mark the end of another day.
They're loyal and true, their love never ends
Skye and Daisy, my four-legged friends.

Aaron Dawber (12)
All Hallows Catholic High School

CHRISTMAS DINNER

It always comes a blunder when Christmas dinner comes to action
And if anything goes wrong, even a fraction
If the mash gets burnt and the peas are multicoloured
But the kids don't care, the kids aren't bothered
All they do is open their presents,
They don't care how the food is unpleasant.
It always comes a blunder when Christmas dinner arrives
And to see the size of the fat meat pies is rather quite grippin'
They always seem to expand, they start off a gentle thing
Until they eat off your hand.
It always comes a blunder when Christmas dinner arrives
When the family turns up with a load of presents
You just want to sit down with a bowl full of refreshments
Christmas dinner always goes wrong
Someone complains the potatoes burnt their tongue.
You've lost the plates
There's a giant list of food people hate.
It always comes a blunder when Christmas dinner arrives
But that's okay it was all a dream
Now let's give the real thing a try.

Rachael Forster (11)
All Hallows Catholic High School

MY LIFE AS WATER

I was born as a trickle of water,
but as I grew up I was rushing down a great, big, massive mountain
passing bridges and villages,
loads of the villagers swam in me because I had no current
but then I started seeing factories
and remembered that they polluted my sister,
I knew I was done for

but then I suddenly swerved to the right
I was heading to a little pond
I was happy but unfortunately I wasn't looking where I was going
and I shot left into the factory, they burned me alive,
now I was forced to make electricity and keep changing form,
first from water then to steam and then back to water
it was so tiring so I went to sleep forever.

Oliver Yates (12)
All Hallows Catholic High School

DARREN

There was a girl called Mary
Who had a yellow canary
She lived in a house
Along with a mouse
And she was quite contrary.

I once had an uncle
Who was called Garfunkle
He lived with Mary
Who he said was quite contrary
And he said that she is scary.

I also have a gran
Who lives with a man
Who likes to eat curds and whey
On a sunny day in May.

Also I have a mum
Who always used to stun
I live with my gran
Along with her man, Stan.

That's my family.

Sinéad Buckley (13)
All Hallows Catholic High School

MY FIRST DAY AT ALL HALLOWS

I packed my bag for school,
checked I had my wallet and keys,
I set off down the lane,
my mum walked down with me.

I caught the bus to school,
went into the playground,
then we went inside
and I had a look around.

At first I felt nervous,
at the end, I felt fine
and then the final bell went,
meaning it's home time.

I got on my bus,
got off at my lane,
then I walked home,
my homework drove me insane.

Jamie Carroll (11)
All Hallows Catholic High School

DREAMLAND

On my way to Dreamland,
I saw a funny man
He had a sack of golden sand
And stripy jim-jams,
He picked up some sand
And chucked it at my eyes,
As soon as my head
Hit the pillow I was asleep,
In Dreamland.

Rebecca Woods (12)
All Hallows Catholic High School

My Animals

Rosie the cat, she's a great big slob,
But she's the cutest cat I've ever had,
She purrs all the time, she sits like a blob
And she's as shy as anything which is sad.
Sammy the cat, well what can I say,
There's not really anything to tell,
He's ginger and stops at two houses in a way,
But he loves us so, oh well.
Pixy the cat whines like a baby
And she's as greedy as a pig,
She runs around the house like a crazy woman, well maybe
And she's 2 now and is quite big.
Holly the dog eats like she's never been fed,
But she probably drinks about a litre a day,
She sleeps so much we should get her a bed,
She's a Newfoundland, but doesn't like water, *okay!*
I have a fish called Bubbles,
I was going to call her Cuddles,
Popeye the fish has eyes like bubbles
And goes around his tank in muddles.
Spliff the cat, the white wuss, all the family call him,
But everyone else calls him Drug,
Cibby the cat, she is a bit dim,
But you just want to give her a hug.
And last, but not least, there's Rambo the cat,
Who looks for the mice he's dug up,
Sometimes he acts like a grumpy, old bat
And other times he's as sweet as a pup.

Gemma Melling (13)
All Hallows Catholic High School

DREAMS

Sometimes my dreams are good
And sometimes they are bad
Sometimes they are happy
And sometimes they are sad.

I like to dream of sweets
And being with my friends
I like to dream of the fun
And the laughter that never ends.

Sometimes I see monsters
Or flashbacks from the past
Whenever I see these visions
I hope they will never last.

Both these dreams seem real
But when I wake they aren't
I wish I understood them
But unfortunately I can't.

Katie Miller (11)
All Hallows Catholic High School

THE TIGER

I like animals big and small,
But the one I think is best of all
Is orange and black with big, sharp claws
And lives on the plains and eats wild boars.

It sleeps in the shade for most of the day
And at night hunts or goes out to play.
Its eyes will see you, wherever you are,
So if you meet it, run far, far, far!

Dominic Bowman (12)
All Hallows Catholic High School

FIREWORK FLASHES!

Up high soaring,
Flames a roaring,
On a wonderful night in November.

The sky is clear,
The whiff is near,
Of scattering shards and smoke.

Chestnuts are roasting,
Feet are toasting,
On a bonfire big and bright.

The scent of burgers, hot dogs and more,
The music of fairground rides galore,
People looking up in amazement.

Grass and mud have been churned,
The locals' wood has been burned,
The guy sitting proud on the top.

The smell and sounds have dropped,
The fire level has dropped,
All gone home.

Stacey Jackson (13)
All Hallows Catholic High School

WINTER

W hite snow drifting slowly down
I   cicles hanging all around
N   ight-time comes, all too soon
T   he fog draws in and creates a gloom
E   verybody collects inside
R   oaring fires we sit beside.

Jessica Marsden (11)
All Hallows Catholic High School

KIDS HEAVEN

What do you think of Heaven?
Do you think it's just up in the sky?
Cos I sometimes wonder,
Is Heaven really way up high?

You know, we could make Heaven as well
And put in all our likes.
Maybe mums and dads, toys and pets
And toss in three or four bikes.

Maybe you're young, a boy or girl
And you like dolls and figures.
Maybe you dream of becoming one day,
A filthy rich, gold mine digger.

We may be able to help you,
Trust us if you care.
We'll try our best to create your dreams
And teach you how to share.

We say to share, cos it makes our Heaven
Really, really nice.
We're not trying to tell you what to do,
We're making our Heaven have that extra spice.

Beth Fraser (11)
All Hallows Catholic High School

BASKETBALL

He came to the court
With his shorts hanging low
The ball of red
A-willing to go
The basket awaiting
For the flying dunk show

He ran to the basket
Flew into the air
And slammed the ball right in there
He got a fifty score
Which gave him the trophy for
The flying dunk show.

Michael Walker (12)
All Hallows Catholic High School

A DAY'S LIKES

I like sugar on my Weetabix
I like a lift to school
I like being early
I like having a discussion in reg
I like a chat on the way to lessons
I like it when we have a practical lesson
I like a snack at break
I like to learn something new
I like being first in the dinner queue
I like the chocolate chip muffins
I like having a laugh with friends
I like planing what to do after school
I like getting top in a test
I like it when it suddenly clicks and I understand everything
I like meeting with friends after school
I like getting a Snickers at Kwik Save
I like going to my friend's house
I like putting on my make-up
I like going out with friends
I like having a sleepover
I like a good night's sleep
I hate getting up early in the morning.

Stephanie Forster (14)
All Hallows Catholic High School

FAMILY FUN!

My family is very large
And our home is seldom quiet,
That's just me being polite
What I mean is it's a riot.

I'll start at the top with my dad
He's the one who earns all the money,
So I suppose that we'll have to put up with
Him thinking that he's so funny.

My mum wears the pants in the house
And keeps us all in line,
She's cool, calm and patient
And scrubs us all till we shine.

The eldest boy is Simon
Who is always singing a song,
But when he goes to uni
He's always gone too long.

Aidy is a fashion freak
Who plays his music loud,
He wears all the trendy gear
To stand out in the crowd.

The middle one is Phillip
Who's obsessed with DIY,
If it's hammering, drilling or just making mess
He's always willing to try.

When there's housework to be done
Alex can be found on the lav,
But I don't mind doing his share
Because he's a good mate to have.

Joseph loves the great outdoors,
Playing in the dirt
And changing the colour of
His nice, clean shirt.

Abigail is the brainy one,
Who plays the violin
And is always complaining about
The way it hurts her chin.

The youngest one is Rosie
Who always has something to say,
It usually ends in screaming
When she doesn't get her own way.

So that is my very big family
And I bet you're all green with envy,
For amongst all the commotion and chaos
Is a home that is loving and friendly.

Lucy Carroll (11)
All Hallows Catholic High School

SCHOOL

School is OK but it drives me round the bend,
With people who think they're the latest trend.
Lessons are fun, some things are cool,
But when you get things wrong you feel like a fool.
Dinner time's a break from things that are hard,
You eat your lunch and play on the yard.
At the end of the day it's time to go home,
But work hasn't finished, you think with a groan.
You want to play out and have some fun,
But you can't go out till homework's done.

Ciaran Barrek (12)
All Hallows Catholic High School

TEENAGERS

There are two teenagers in my home,
They love to stamp, sulk and moan,
They yell and scream and slam the doors,
Stamp about on the upstairs floors!

They play loud music deep into the night,
When they go out they look a sight,
They have to have the latest trends,
It drives my mother round the bend!

Shopping's a thing they like to do
And hanging out with all the 'crew',
On mobile phones they can talk for ages,
I think they should be locked up in cages!

Now I'm getting worried about myself,
The thing is I'm nearly twelve,
I'm down in the dumps, I'm feeling blue,
Mums says soon I'll be a teenager too!

Emily Hatsell (11)
All Hallows Catholic High School

WITCHCRAFT

A slimy tail from a scaly rat
A beady eye from a ginger cat
A big fat bull's gooey brain
The king of the jungle's hairy mane.

A waxy head from an earwig
Woolly ears from a clumsy pig
Woodlouse from a rotting box
A scarred paw from a deadly fox.

Natasha Fowler (13)
All Hallows Catholic High School

RED

Red is anger
Red is rage
Red will grow on you as you age

Red will tear your life in two
Red will drive your sanity away
Until you figure out what to do

Pain and sorrow, plea and whim
Are all included in this din
Passion, love, hate and pain
Are all things in this lesson you'll gain

Learn to live with
Or ignore some emotions
And then you'll understand
Life's cruel motions.

Emma Clapham (14)
All Hallows Catholic High School

WINTER'S DAY

Grass flowing by,
Robins singing a sweet lullaby,
Sun blazing in the sky,
The coldness of the breeze,
The crunchy frosty leaves,
Squirrels scampering up the trees.
Snow falling in the breeze,
Branches snapping off the trees,
Children running in the wind,
Blue tits' branches being pinned.

Stephanie Smith (12)
All Hallows Catholic High School

PETS

I'll sing a song about some pets
One of which went to the vets
After going for a test
He went up my vest
He's a real pest
As he failed his IQ test
He wasn't a fake
He was a real snake
He was a real pest
And he's up my vest

I'll sing a song about some pets
One of which had to go to the vets
Some are scary some are hairy
Some are lumpy and some are bumpy

The other little critter
Never gave me a rash
Never bit me and never
Harmed my stash
He keeps real still
But he can move lightning fast
Waits for his prey
Then pounces at last
He sucks it dry
Like a piece of rye
He throws it away
And calls it a day

I'll tell you a song about some pets
One of which went to the vets
Some are scary some are hairy
Some are lumpy and some are bumpy

And the other day I played follow the leader
I was a believer and
He was the leader
He's as sly as a fox
And as brazen as an ox
He treats my home like his own ghetto
Yes, you've guessed it, he's a leopard gecko.

Peter Gartland (12)
All Hallows Catholic High School

HOPES AND FEELINGS

First day at my new school
Children line up straight
Uniform without a crease
Graffiti by the gate.

Whispers on each corner
Fingers pointing low
Booming voices mellow
To tell them where to go.

Corridors without bending
Travel through the gloom
Polished floors lead the way
To another paint-chipped room.

Faces unfamiliar
Turn the other way
To hide for good the memories
And thoughts from my first day.

Nicola Young (11)
All Hallows Catholic High School

A POEM FOR MY AUNTIE ALI!

We think about her every day
and in every single kind of way!
She will always be stood right by our sides,
Our feelings for her we can never hide.

She never said, 'Why am I the one to suffer this disease?'
But more concerned to put everyone first and completely at their ease.

Lord, did you take her, is it true?
You need a gorgeous, loving angel in Heaven with you.

She was a fantastic mum and friend to all,
Her family is trying to be brave and standing tall.

We miss her now, but it won't be long till we see her smiley face,
Up in Heaven she now waits happily, saving us all a space.

She is no longer in pain and has no fears
about the cancer she had to fight.
We want her to know she is so special and she's in our thoughts,
hearts and prayers at night.

We now all have to get on with our lives,
she wouldn't want us to make a big fuss.
Because now deep inside we all know
Ali will be watching over us!

Natalie Webb (13)
All Hallows Catholic High School

PLEASE MUM CAN I HAVE A DOG?

Please Mum can I have a dog?
I promise to walk him, feed him, everything, honest.
Please Mum can I have a dog?
I've never wanted something so much.
Please Mum can I have a dog?

Please Mum can I have a dog?
When I'm lonely and sad I will have something to keep me company.
Please Mum can I have a dog?
If you let me I promise I'll never ask for anything again.
Please Mum can I have a dog?

Thomas Addison (11)
All Hallows Catholic High School

CHOCOLATE

C   hocolate is the thing to eat,
    when you're feeling like a treat.

H   ow we love our chocolate bars,
    Time Out, Wispa, Crunchie, Mars.

O   ther snacks are not as good,
    chocolate beats them, as it should!

C   hocolate is the food of dreams,
    filled with nuts, toffees and creams.

O   h I could eat chocolate, all day long,
    but to eat too much, could that be wrong?

L   ick your lips and have a feast,
    eat 20 chocolate bars at least!

A   ero, Flake, Yorkie, Dream,
    if I can't have chocolate, I think I'll scream!

T   wix, Galaxy, KitKat too,
    coming to a supermarket, near you!

E   veryone loves chocolate, of this there is no doubt,
    it makes me feel so happy, I just want to shout!

Alexandra Gibbons (11)
All Hallows Catholic High School

GRANDAD

As angels keep their watch up there,
Please God just let him know,
That we down here will not forget
We love and miss him so.

He left so suddenly
His last thoughts unknown,
But he left special memories,
We are so proud to own.

It's been a lonely time without you
And nothing is the same,
All we have are memories
And pictures in a frame.

You hold a special spot, deep in my heart,
Where the sun will always shine,
For there will never be another to me,
Like that wonderful grandfather of mine.

A place in our hearts no one can fill,
We miss you Grandad and always will.

Stacy Bashall (13)
All Hallows Catholic High School

SIGNS OF HALLOWE'EN

Witch's broom
Dark and gloom
Moonlight shines bright
Wolves howl in the night.

Devil daring
House haunting
Ghosts swim in midnight air
Witches cackle in their lair.

Vampire jaws
Monster claws
Nothing to fear?
Hallowe'en's here!

Kelly Roddy (11)
All Hallows Catholic High School

CAUGHT OUT LUKE

I have to think of a poem for school,
But I don't know what to do it on.
If I don't do it I'll look a fool,
'Cause I'd be the only one without one.

So, I know, I'll write the title 'Pink'
And then leave the page blank.
Then when Miss asks,
I'll say, 'But it's invisible ink.'

I left the poem far too late
And didn't have time to sleep.
I was still tired as I walked through the school gate,
So I suddenly began to weep.

As the day went on by,
I could hardly do any work at all.
I knew that I still had to try,
Otherwise I'd feel small.

'Stand up Luke and read your poem,'
'Please Miss I feel sick, can I go home?'
I got caught out but learnt the lesson,
Teachers aren't fools, they're not for messin'!

Luke Henry (11)
All Hallows Catholic High School

MONSTERS IN MY BEDROOM

There's monsters in my bedroom
They come out every night
They're hidden in there all day long
Until I turn out the light

There's one that lies beneath my bed
With a long, thin, scaly back
Inch-long claws and powerful legs
Waiting, ready to attack

The shadow monster on my bed
Sat there, he's really creepy
I've got to try to stay awake
He'll get me when I get sleepy

The wardrobe monster he's the worst
Hands visible on the door
The door creaks open and out he comes
Prowling across the floor

The window monster on the sill
Hidden behind the curtain
Moving slowly, not making a sound
I know he's there for certain

There's monsters in my bedroom
They come out every night
They're hidden in there all day long
Until I turn out the light.

Richard O'Sullivan (12)
All Hallows Catholic High School

MY BIG BRO

Errr he's visiting again
Cleaning out the fridge
Driving me insane
My big brother - what a pain!

He thinks he's all cool and neat
From head to cheesy feet
Well the rest of us don't agree
You wouldn't get him near me

He always argues and makes me mad
Then we get shouted at by Mum and Dad
'It's all her fault,' he says
I'll get him back one of these days . . .

Oh he's going home now and I get his room
I really hope he decides not to visit again soon
But if he does I'll get out
Go to my friends, I won't hang about

Well at least he's gone
But we have no more food
Sometimes he's so selfish and always rude

At the end of the day
I'm glad he's gone away
But I want you to know
He's still my big bro.

Kate Sedgwick (13)
All Hallows Catholic High School

JOURNEY

I am a trickle of water
Rushing down the hillside.
Pebbles and stones I carry with me,
Over the rapids and rocks I go.

Now I am a stream
Over the rocks then . . .
Splash! Crash!
Over a waterfall for the very first time.
The froth at the bottom is white and clean.

Now I am bigger,
Look I'm a river.
I go through a valley and into the town,
My sack of stones have dropped.
I am smooth and sparkly clean.

Now I am at the end of the river and coming to the sea,
I am very calm,
As calm as can be.
Remember, I go on forever.

Lucy Jackson (13)
All Hallows Catholic High School

STRANDED

There was a young girl stranded at sea
Who fell and bashed her knee
She was not amused
Then she blew a fuse
And said, 'Oh deary me!'
Once she was down
You'd never guess what she had found
It was a big, flat gun covered in gum.

Later a plane went by
She shot her flare, but only to stare
The plane was in a flame
Then she said, 'Oh deary me!'

Matthew Bradley (13)
All Hallows Catholic High School

THE WRITER OF THIS POEM
(Based on 'The Writer of This Poem' by Roger McGough')

The writer of this poem
Is as strong as a tree
As cunning as a fox
And as quick as a bee

As bright as the stars
As happy as the sun
As wise as an owl
And is really, really fun

As fluffy as a cloud
As cute as a cat
As funny as a clown
And as flat as a mat

As silly as a sausage
As mad as a hatter
As hot as fire
And she always natters

The writer of this poem is simply the best
You couldn't beat this poem because she's already beaten the rest.

Abigail Testa (11)
All Hallows Catholic High School

MY PETS

At the age of five-ish I soon decided
I wanted a tarantula,
Big and hairy,
He had to be a lean, mean, killing machine
And don't forget very scary.
On my sixth,
What a gift,
I happily got my huge spider.
But on my seventh it was different,
For what I desired was a long and slippery serpent.
I got it, I got it,
My own giant royal python
And yes he was definitely in charge,
He was long, strong with a pointed forked tongue
And an appetite which was terribly large.
If you like strange animals,
Like me,
There's nothing to be feared.
No matter how big, long, strange and
Strong and creepy, wonderful and weird.

Sam Bond (13)
All Hallows Catholic High School

MY KITE

It flies through the sky,
With the strength of the wind.
It glides like a plane,
Past the drizzling rain.
It dips low to the ground,
To whisper a sound.
Then climbs high in the sky,
With a long, loud sigh.

With the wings of a bird,
It looks quite absurd.
Dancing with glee,
Performing splendidly.
The colour's bold and bright,
It's such a fantastic sight
To see me flying
My enchanting kite.

Sophie Nisbet (13)
All Hallows Catholic High School

I WILL ALWAYS REMEMBER

I wish I knew you better,
But now my chance has gone.
Although this day moves slowly,
Time will still go on.

I hold my head down,
As a gesture of respect.
I hope you remember me,
In fact you will, I bet.

When I heard the sad news,
That you had passed away,
I realised life wasn't always happy,
That sad and cold day.

There's a very special way of remembering you
And a very special part.
I always will remember you,
At the bottom of my heart.

Olivia Stringfellow (13)
All Hallows Catholic High School

HALLOWE'EN

Hallow'een, Hallowe'en, Hallowe'en
You're sure to have a great scream.
You're likely to see skeletons,
Witches and vampires everywhere
Even Frankenstein with green hair.

You can trick and treat in the street
The night is dark and gloomy.
Pumpkins are burning brightly
Their scary faces glowing.

At home the party has just begun,
Spooky games, dances, murder mysteries
Are really fun!

The end of the night is here.
Oh no! Never mind I'll wait until next year.

Lewis Blanchard (11)
All Hallows Catholic High School

THE TOAD AND THE FLY

I was walking down the road
And then I saw a toad,
The toad saw a fly,
Jumped into the sky,
They went through my eye,
They came out of my ear,
I could not hear,
I fell on the floor and said,
'Why, why, why do I have to die?'
From that silly little toad and the fly.

Ollie Ashley (11)
All Hallows Catholic High School

THE OLD MAN AND HIS DOG

He was sad and old,
He was lanky and bold,
He was locked away in an old, abandoned house.

He had a great big clock,
Which went *tick, tick, tock.*

He also had a dog,
Which was sad and old.

He ate his dinner with a spoon
And then he would stare at the moon.

He did this all day until he and his dog,
Finally passed away.

James Dally (13)
All Hallows Catholic High School

WEATHER

It's raining,
It's snowing,
The sun is glowing
And the rainbow is in the sky.

It's a beautiful day,
It's a horrible day,
Which is going to stay.

The snow, the rain,
Such terrible pain,
Frost nipping at my fingers.

I love the weather whatever it is,
But please sun don't go away!

Ryan Jones (11)
All Hallows Catholic High School

MY WISHES

I wish I could win everything,
I wish I could run like the wind,
I really wish I could sing,
I wish I was brilliant at everything.

I wish I was top of the class,
I wish at everything I could pass.
I wish I was good at writing things.
I wish I was good at history, English and French.

I wish I was a millionaire,
I wish I had really nice hair,
I wish I was the prettiest girl in school,
I wish I was really cool.

Do you want to know what I really wish . . . ?
I wish I was you!

Steph Hammel (13)
All Hallows Catholic High School

FOOTBALL

Football is my passion
We play other teams and thrash 'em
My team is called Penny Boys
Whose colour is blue and red
We are a good team I've heard it said
As we pass the ball down the field
To score yet another
The crowd is shouting and cheering
But the loudest is my mother
The game is won 7-2
And now to the next round we're through.

Andrew Wood (12)
All Hallows Catholic High School

BEST FRIENDS

B   est friends are really cool,
E   specially if they go to your school,
S   ometimes you have 1 or 3,
T   he best thing is that they're free.

F   riends are forever,
R   emember they are,
I   f you don't, they're not there
E   veryone together
N   ever forget,
D   oing things together is something you should do
S   illy things and stupid things is the best thing too.

Sarah Topping (12)
All Hallows Catholic High School

MY DOG GINGER

My dog Ginger,
Is brown and white.
He is very small,
But very bright.

He has little flappy ears
And a wiggly, waggly tail.
When he plays in the garden,
He eats all the snails.

But the best thing about Ginger,
Has to be,
That I love him
And he loves me.

Francesca Pladgeman (11)
All Hallows Catholic High School

THE BULLY

As I walked down the street,
I dreaded our meeting
The things you say
I was terrified of the day
When we would meet
Beyond the street
Will you punch?
Will I crunch?
When the fists meet the face
Will I bleed?
Will I die?
Will I have time to say, 'Goodbye?'

Katie Tyrer (13)
All Hallows Catholic High School

SKATEBOARDING

Skateboarding is fun,
Skateboarding is cool,
Kick-flips, heel-flips,
Ollies and 360 flips,
Are some of many tricks,
You can try,
There are challenges
Everywhere for a skater,
At a park, on the street,
Even a wall will do,
Magazines and videos
Will teach you what to do.

Matthew Smith (12)
All Hallows Catholic High School

WARNINGS AND CAUTIONS

We live in a world full of warnings,
Cautions telling us what not to do,
But what if these warnings were not here?
People would have to look after themselves,
Judge for themselves whether something is safe,
Nobody could break the rules.
But nobody could abide by them.
Is it possible to imagine?
Being able to climb electricity pylons,
Going the wrong way on what was a one-way road,
Would this be better?
Most probably not.
People would constantly have accidents,
Be in trouble, be 'wrongdoing'.

Next time you complain at a road sign
Or a warning sign,
Remember that it's there for a reason.

Adam Mercer (13)
All Hallows Catholic High School

MY BIRTHDAY

My birthday's in the middle of May,
It really is a special day.
My presents stacked up high,
The time just flies by.
For my last birthday I got lots and lots,
Including a book full of dot to dots.
I can't wait for my next birthday in the middle of May!

Aileen Scott (11)
All Hallows Catholic High School

FROM MY POINT OF VIEW . . .

Being as I'm a teenager, I've got a right to moan,
So I'm going to write about the things that make me groan.

I hate the way I'm always told, what's good from what is bad,
Why can't people realise, their moaning makes me mad?
Why when I ask a question, do I never get an answer?
Like, why does Father Christmas have a reindeer called Prancer?

Why am I always criticised, if I share out my ideas
Or if I make a sarcastic comment about Prince Charles' ears?
Why am I happy, then suddenly depressed?
And what is it with old men and those ridiculous string vests?

Why do old ladies have their hair rinsed pink and blue?
And why do men grow beards? I don't have a clue.
Why do I never have enough clothes, although my cupboard's full?
And why does my frizzy hair always look so dull?

Why do people only ever judge you by your looks?
And why do fairy tales only come true in books?
Why are some celebrities so spiteful and stroppy?
And why does my handwriting always look so sloppy?

Why do some things make me go insane?
And how can snooker be called a game?
Why do I hate being so tall?
And why does this poem make no sense at all?

Oh, I know, because it was written by me
And I'm the one, the only, Ali C!
I'm totally crazy and mental too,
I'm passionate about my feelings, how about you?

Alison Criddle (13)
All Hallows Catholic High School

SCHOOL

School has many different lessons
And they're all split into different sessions,
In all the lessons you're always working,
There is not enough time for chatting and smirking.

In English you do many things,
Comprehensions, drama and essays
And if you're really good at this,
You could soon be starring in a couple of plays.

Maths is also a busy lesson,
Graphs, polygons, sequences and patterns,
Some people say that these are easy,
But I just think that they are being really cheesy.

French is another one of those things,
Bonjour, bon soir and je m'appelle,
These are only the main basics,
It is very hard to learn these well.

Geography isn't as easy as it looks,
Reservoirs, mountains, and parts of land.
In geography you colour and draw a lot,
So all the time you'll be using your hands.

History is what some say is boring,
Henry VIII and World War I.
Most of it is all about kings,
But you learn everything that's happened under the sun.

PE is what most say is the best lesson,
Football, netball and badminton,
All the time you have much fun,
These are good to play when there's a nice sun.

Daniel Porter (12)
All Hallows Catholic High School

THE MEANING OF CHRISTMAS

Tinsel hanging in the hall,
Turkey's ready on the table,
Christmas tree stood proud and tall,
Baby Jesus in the stable.

Relatives arrive from far away,
Grandma's starting on the sherry,
Everyone's happy it's Christmas Day,
It's the one time of year everyone's merry!

Presents 'neath the Christmas tree,
The Queen is speaking on the telly,
Everyone's full, no room for tea,
Grandad sits back and pats his belly.

Santa Claus has been and gone,
Had a drink and ate his pie,
Left lots of gifts for everyone,
Off he goes across the sky.

All that's left is Christmas cake,
A few cold sprouts and dirty dishes,
Then we see the first snowflake,
Everyone's had their Christmas wishes.

Christmas is about Jesus' love,
Amongst all the presents, we seem to forget,
Now he's gone and he's high above,
I wonder if anyone's realised yet?

Jess Heaney (13)
Archbishop Temple School

CHRISTMAS

The tree is up and gleaming,
Standing like a mountain tall,
The presents underneath it,
There'll soon be none at all.

The turkey's on the table,
Scrumptious, steaming and still,
We'd better eat it quick though,
Cos here comes Uncle Bill.

Bill bustles in,
With presents for us all,
Like Santa with his sack,
He's round, he's fat, he's small.

For Martin there's a skateboard,
A bat and ball for Ben,
For Mum and Dad some brandy
And for me a nice new pen.

The snow outside is falling,
It's cold, it's fluffy, it's white,
Small children's faces glow,
In wonder and delight.

Christmas is nearly over
And now it's getting late,
Faces tired and gloomy,
Another year to wait.

Stefanie Billing (14)
Archbishop Temple School

CHRISTMAS IS NEARLY HERE

Snow is falling lightly,
It's almost Christmas Day,
Snowmen built up slightly,
Excitement's on its way.
On street corners, Christmas carols are sung,
Inside different houses, Christmas decorations are hung.
Robins fly around in the cold winter breeze,
People all around watch their car windows freeze.
Christmas trees are put up,
Standing tall and proud,
With the children playing and laughing very loud,
Turkeys are bought.
Fighting over toys, it's on its way,
People are getting ready,
Ready for Christmas Day.

Stockings are being hung,
Above the fire warm,
In a few days,
Is the day when Jesus was born.

Hayley Jones (13)
Archbishop Temple School

CHRISTMAS

Soft snow falls gently
On the rooftop
Christmas lights gleam brightly
In the Christmas tree shop

Presents are being opened
By children smiling with glee
While the adults have just tucked
Into a large turkey

All the wine has been poured
And all the people are drunk
The fireworks have all exploded
Another Christmas has gone and the lights are out in a blink.

Jonathan Murrin (14)
Archbishop Temple School

POETRY NATURE

Autumn, winter, summer and spring, each season turns into
another world.
Every animal and plant, every little thing has a life of its own.
It's a green world, wrapped in a bubble of blue sky and that dot of gold.
It's a haven filled with life; plants weave through each other
like they're sewn.
Animals run around exploring the greens, purple, yellow and brown
of their world.

The ground like a carpet of green, sweeps through the trees in and out.
It's as if a green giant walked across and turned everything green.
Out of the ground the plants sprout.
Animals dart away from the outside, not daring to be seen.
Another world unspoilt, untouched, not wanting to share,
another world just there.

Trees sway to and fro swaying in the breeze,
Like dancing figures they dance.
Animals' ears pricked up at the slightest sound they freeze,
Looking for a sign of danger at first glance.

Flowers grow in the fields,
Yellow, purple, red, green and red,
Growing around the trees protecting them like a shield.
Mind working, heart beating, always breathing, never dead.

Samantha Cheyne (13)
Archbishop Temple School

It's Christmas!

It's Christmas and the birds are singing,
It's Christmas and the church bells are ringing,
It's Christmas and the snow is white,
Don't go outside or you will get frostbite.

It's Christmas and the tree is green,
It's Christmas be kind not mean,
It's Christmas and the lights are bright,
Don't go outside or you will get frostbite.

It's Christmas and there are lots of presents,
It's Christmas eat turkeys not pheasants,
It's Christmas there are no cars in sight,
Don't go outside or you will get frostbite.

It's Christmas and the music is thudding,
It's Christmas let's eat Christmas pudding,
It's Christmas and my bro has got a new kite,
Don't go outside or you will get frostbite.

It's Christmas and the air is cold,
It's Christmas and my dad is bald,
When I heard the front door closing I got quite a fright,
It was my sister and guess what she had . . .
frostbite!

Anthony Pape (13)
Archbishop Temple School

Christmas Eve

As the day closes like a chilly May, Christmas
Yes it's on its way.
With glistening lights, all sparkling and bright,
Upstairs the family silently, soundly sleep.
While back outside, the people are about.
The adults walking, the young teens talking.

86

In what in our day was an ice-covered May.
And back inside, the children wait . . .
Wait . . . wait for a visitor, a man, a friend.
The little ones listen to footsteps, but who could it be?
The chimes are ringing, the young are singing
And back in the house, they wait for that special friend.

Rebecca Stuart (13)
Archbishop Temple School

BONFIRE NIGHT

Fountains sprayed blue and red,
While rockets whizzed overhead.
Fireworks flew,
Crowds grew,
On that Bonfire Night.

Sparklers glittered green and gold,
Waved around by young and old.
Rockets zoomed,
Bangers boomed,
On that Bonfire Night.

The fire burned. Sizzled. Smoked,
With giant logs it was stoked.
Fireworks flew,
Crowds grew,
On that Bonfire Night.

Treacle toffee was eaten away,
Crying children who wanted to stay.
Rockets zoomed,
Bangers boomed,
On that Bonfire Night.

Ricky McCann (13)
Archbishop Temple School

CELEBRATION

Around this time every year
The autumn leaves turn brown
But these months just melt away
And the pantos pull out the clown.

Around this time every year
We find a time to celebrate
For Christmas time is nearly here
And again we'll overrate it.

But through this time we must ask
A question of great need
Is this time really good
Or is it ruled by greed?

But there are people here who need us
And thousands die each year
With no one there to care for us
Oh yeah! It's Christmas cheer!

I think that now I've told you
I hope you'll stop and wonder
If you can help these people
Yes, it's time to face the thunder.

So here's a poem on celebration
But, please do not forget,
Those people who are alone this year
Those people who face neglect.

Judi Holmes (13)
Archbishop Temple School

CELEBRATE WITH ME

I walk upon the street
And ask whomever I may meet,
To sing and dance,
To shout and prance
And celebrate with me.

Don't just stand
Upon this blissful land,
Don't stop the pace,
For every day's a race,
To celebrate with me.

No need to stay in line,
It's free to have a good time,
I can feel the excitement,
The drawing enticement,
So celebrate with me.

What are you waiting for?
It's party time for sure,
If I stretch up high,
I can touch the sky,
Please celebrate with me.

What is the reason? I hear you call
No reason, I reply, none at all,
It's not every day
You're alive to say,
Come celebrate with me!

Harriet Carr (13)
Archbishop Temple School

I LOVE CHRISTMAS!

I love Christmas,
It's my favourite time of year!
All the presents, big and small,
Maybe it's a bouncing ball!
It could be a brand new hat
Or a gorgeous pussy cat!

I love Christmas,
It's my favourite time of year!

Everything covered like icing on a cake,
Tracks looking just like a snake.
'Let's build a snowman, round and fat,
He can have my bobble hat.'

I love Christmas,
It's my favourite time of year!

But when it's all over . . .
I look forward to October.
Leaves crunching on the ground,
Autumn appearing all around.

But I still love Christmas,
It's my favourite time of year!

Isobel Holgeth (12)
Archbishop Temple School

THE WEDDING

Happy, this was the mood in the church,
Happy, these were the tears of the bride,
Happy, were the smiles of the groom,
Happy, were the humorous tones of the best man,
Happy, was the crying of the bride's dad.

Happy, were the faces on the glass windows,
Happy, was the chirping of the birds outside,
Happy, were the elaborate paintings on the ceiling,
Happy, were the stuffed guests.

Happy, was the wedding!

Jonathan Clayton (12)
Archbishop Temple School

POEM

I was told today,
my family was careless,
I was told today,
my family was worthless.

I was told today,
my family didn't share,
I was told today,
my family didn't care.

I was told today,
my family was cruel,
I was told today,
my family wasn't crucial.

I was told today,
my family didn't matter,
I was told today,
my family was a scatter.

I told them today,
that they were wrong,
and all you need is family,
wherever you're from.

Amiee Harrison-Armstrong (13)
Archbishop Temple School

A NEW BABY

A new baby has been born,
So there is not time to mourn.
Come over here to have a look,
But bring a magnifying glass cause he's the size of a puck!

Now the baby is a year old,
Even though he's still bald.
He's getting clever day by day,
But his favourite word is still, 'Hey!'

The toddler is now two years of age,
We've started keeping him in a playpen.
His favourite food is sausage and mash,
He'll even buy it with his own cash.

The child is now three years old,
His hair is starting to look like mould.
He's starting to act really cool,
But his favourite animal is still a mule!

The kid is now four years of age.
He's on his way to school
And I think he's forgotten about me and the mule.

Sam Reader (12)
Archbishop Temple School

THE WEDDING

The guests all arrive looking fine,
The groom is nervous and asks the time.
The organist plays yet another hymn,
Why does he bother with all the din?

The vicar slowly walks to the altar,
The bride and her father try not to falter.
Bridesmaids follow close behind clutching
Their flowers of every kind.

The service soon ends, confetti is thrown,
But with the strong wind, away it's blown.
Off to the reception for a good do,
Everyone's happy, newly-weds too.

James Hindle (12)
Archbishop Temple School

NEW YEAR'S EVE!

We are all dancing
And singing too.
The minutes left are
Twenty-two!

The food's all gone
The crisps as well
The music plays,
As loud as hell!

The minutes left
Are only ten
The countdown starts . . .
We watch Big Ben!

The bubbly's out
We gather round
And wait to hear
That famous sound.

One minute left
The bubbly's poured,
Now listen to that
Great, big *roar*

Happy New Year!

Rachel Botes (12)
Archbishop Temple School

CHRISTMAS

Christmas is an excuse for decoration,
A great time for celebration,.
Underneath the Christmas tree
Are presents waiting for you and me.

Outside the soft snow blows into homes,
To lonely people on their own.
The flashing lights make fantastic sights,
Full of smiles and empty isles.
Christmas is an excuse for decoration,
A great time for celebration.

Inside the smell of turkey rises,
Into the room filled with prizes.
Children's faces burst with happiness,
Which make sup for people filled with sadness.
Christmas is an excuse for decoration,
A great time for celebration.

Sleigh bells ring as carol singers sing
And party people play with silly string.
You can hear people screaming,
While others are dreaming,
For Santa to come back
With a huge red sack.

Christmas is an excuse for decoration,
A great time for celebration.

Lisa Hull (13)
Archbishop Temple School

CELEBRATION

Palms are sweaty,
Heart one beat ahead,
Breath deeper,
Blood rushing to head,
Feel faint,
Feel dizzy,
Nerves are
Very busy,
Waiting in suspense,
My name called out,
Cheers fill the air,
Whistles and shouts
Are everywhere,
I've done it,
I've come out on top,
I've succeeded,
I don't want to stop,
Everyone clapping,
Smile on my face,
Heart still beating,
One extra pace,
The others are full
Of aggravation,
I think this calls
For a celebration.

Amanda Horton (13)
Archbishop Temple School

MY GRANNY'S BIRTHDAY

My granny's had her hair done,
She's had it done bright red
She's had it dyed
So it will hide,
The grey bits on her head!

My granny started yoga
She wiggles on the floor
And ties herself up in knots
My granny is no bore!

My granny started swimming,
She takes me to the pool
While I just flap, she does front crawl
And makes me feel a fool!

My granny's really trendy
At the disco she's a wow!
The problem is, she seems to be
Much younger than me now!

Jessica Hunter (12)
Archbishop Temple School

BIRTHDAYS

It's your birthday coming soon,
It's your birthday, I'll get the balloons.
We'll be as happy as can be,
Come on Mum, just you and me.

Come on Mum, we'll show them all,
Come on Mum, we'll have a ball.
Please Mum, let's celebrate,
Mum, it will be great.

At one point I thought you had lost your marbles,
But now I see you never had any to start with.
You and me,
Not clever, not dumb,
But you and me,
Are still number one.

Lindsay Latibeaudiere (12)
Archbishop Temple School

CHRISTMAS

Autumn is slowly blowing away,
Making way for winter.
Red and gold glows crumpling up,
Frosty nights growing dimmer.

Tiny flakes of snow are fluttering down,
Pitter-pattering softly off the ground.
Gorgeous smells of warm mince pies, come drifting up to the sky,
Ready for tomorrow when the family arise.

Ripping sounds erupt into the early morning air,
As children open Christmas presents with very little care.
Church bells are ringing and the choirboys are singing,
Celebrating the birth of our true king.

Christmas lunch awaits for the family after church
And little Johnny red bird sits on his little perch.

Christmas trees now exploding with thousands of fairy lights,
Children begin to close their eyes
And dream with delight.
As stars zoom around the galaxy,
They remember the real story
How at Christmas, Jesus was born.

Rebecca L Keating (12)
Archbishop Temple School

BLACK

Black, what is it?
Black is a smothering sound,
Black is darkness all around.
Black is death,
Can black be beauty?
I wonder if
Black can be beauty, like a panther.
But then black can be a gloomy day when the world crashes down;
An evil man or a storm.
Black is muffled and can hardly be heard,
Sounds like drowning and crying out for help, but can't.
What puzzles me is . . .
Can black be death, with babies crying, nothing to see
And hot then cold but black not making his mind up?
Or
Can black be a wondrous place with mystery,
With the silver moon and blackberries to eat?
Black is not blue nor brown but unique
Black is murky seaweed and big scares.
When the lights go out black is back!

Sita Bridglal (12)
Archbishop Temple School

HALLOWE'EN

At the end of October falls Hallowe'en,
A time when the dead rise all pale and green.
The pumpkins glow in the black night sky,
You know that tonight someone will die!

The witches cackle over their broth,
An eye of a newt, a wing of a moth.
The vampire's teeth glint in the light
They turn into bats and fly off out of sight!

The night carries on with more screams and cries,
Until people go home and the atmosphere dies.
The dead are reburied; the ghosts laid to rest,
This Hallowe'en was definitely the best!

Victoria Holden (12)
Archbishop Temple School

CELEBRATION

Christmas is a time to celebrate
We are joyful and our hearts are full of warmth
A time when friends and family come together.

Christmas is a time to celebrate
The putting out of decorations
The Christmas tree all shining bright,
Like a star in the night's sky.

Christmas is a time to celebrate.
The butterflies in your stomach,
You are wanting to go to sleep but you can't.

Christmas is a time to celebrate
Children are as happy as can be
Smothered from head to toe with presents.

Christmas is a time to celebrate
We celebrate the birth of Jesus.

Christmas is a time to celebrate
The taking down of decorations
Christmas is coming to an end
This is the end of our celebration.

Samantha Dorrington (12)
Archbishop Temple School

RED!

What is red?
Red is a squirrel
And a ruby twinkling in the sun.
An apple
And anger bubbling up like a volcano
And flames as a building blows up,
with lots of innocent people inside.
Red is the colour of Liverpool's shirts
And a pepper in a hot chilli.
Red is walking into a room and being
surrounded by people shouting.
And it's a *crash* as a car collides with another.
Red is blood bleeding as fast as you can run
and bullies crowding round you and pushing
you into a corner
and a person blushing as they are kissed.
Red is a beautiful, calm poppy
and a warm fire in your living room.
Red
Said
Bed
they fled!

Jennifer Brown (12)
Archbishop Temple School

BLUE

Blue is sadness
And rain and the sky and water that I can swim in.
Blue is bluebottles crawling around and dolphins and whales.
Blue is coldness and ice and ink.
Blue is like a blue lagoon and puddles and rivers and streams.
Blue is waterfalls.
Blue is the smell of blueberry pie and a sunny sky.

Blue is darkness and sapphire stones
And moans and groans.
Blue is like the waves of the sea
And the whistling of the wind
And calmness.

Sarah Allen (12)
Archbishop Temple School

RED

Red is a fox
And a devil in a cave
And a heart-shaped flower
And a puddle of blood
Spilled in an alley.
Red is
Ouch
A fire,
A cherry,
A strawberry.
Red makes me feel scared
Lonely and fierce
Red makes me feel angry
And alone.
Red is a hot barbecue.
Red is a place deep in the mountains
Where the hawks live deep in the forest
Hidden in my dream.
Red is love, friendship
And sunset.
Red is autumn
And the red leaves.
Red is Comic Relief
And plenty of mischief.

Chloe Anderton (12)
Archbishop Temple School

SPRING!

The days of winter have swiftly gone,
Like a switch on the wall going off and on,
They go by my eyes in a flash.

When I rise in the early morning,
All of the baby birds are calling
And the bees buzz quickly by the window.

I know that it's spring again,
Because God has stopped the rain
And the sun can now come out from the clouds.

Fine is the spring weather,
It brings nature and people together,
On picnics out in the park.

The fields are like a carpet of green,
Everything is fresh and clean,
All the daisies stand tall and proud.

Nestling in the trees,
Swaying gently in the breeze,
The buds sit waiting to emerge.

Spring lambs stand in the fields without care,
They bound and leap into the air,
Don't you think it's a wonderful sight to see.

This is such a beautiful season,
I wrote this poem for that reason,
To *celebrate the spring!*

Rebecca Calvert (13)
Archbishop Temple School

MY BIRTHDAY

I wake up and I get out of bed
14 years to this day I was born
and I've changed a lot in the course of my life.

When I started out I didn't really know
What was going on or what was happening
14 years ago to this day,
14 years ago to this day.

I was a toddler and I lived in my own world,
I learned what my legs and lips were for,
12 years ago to this day,
12 years ago to this day.

My brother had been born and I was so content!
My brother was born and I was so lucky!
10 years ago to this day,
10 years ago to this day.

Then I left school to start my new life
At that Castle High School,
3 years ago to this day,
3 years ago to this day.

Now I'm a teen and I'm growing
All the time, fast, fast, fast,
On this day,
On this day.

It's my birthday,
Today's my birthday.
It's my birthday,
I'm 14 today.

Luke Healey (13)
Archbishop Temple School

GREEN

Green is as large as a field on a farm,
An apple picked freshly from a tree.
Green is
e
n
v
y
And a walk in the woods,
Where I relax and
daydream!
Green is the sound of the wind rustling through
the trees
Whoosh! Whoosh!
Green is an emerald twinkling in the warm sun,
A green grape bush, growing in Greece!
Green is a cool summer breeze
And the smell of a freshly mowed lawn.

Kerrie Bath (12)
Archbishop Temple School

MY CELEBRATION POEM

Celebration is a time of joy,
As it greets the birth of every girl and boy.
Celebration is a time of goodwill,
When we can forget about the bill.
Celebration comes and goes,
Just as we start to enjoy it
It leaves for a year or two.

Christmas is when the snow comes out
And all the little children sing and shout.
We build snowmen and have snow fights,
Then we go inside for chipolata bites.

Birthdays are when we look back on another year gone
And our parents get the con.
We can stuff our faces
And enjoy the races,
Then it is all gone.

Helen Worrall (12)
Archbishop Temple School

CELEBRATION POEM

Like the bang of a drum,
the party poppers start.
Celebration is here,
laughter in our hearts.

Lights flashing everywhere
like a sparkling star-studded sky.
The turkey dinner arrives
glasses are raised high.

The slosh of champagne,
the smell of the food.
Everything you look at
puts you in a jolly mood.

The tree glistens silently,
we sing of Christmas cheer.
Everyone's excited
and looking forward to New Year.

Presents all opened,
it's getting late,
you look around your empty plate
for any remains of Christmas Day,
yet for another year, it's gone away.

Sophie Dean (14)
Archbishop Temple School

THE WEDDING

I entered the church through the old oak door,
A trail of pale lilies are on all sides of the floor.
They twirl and wrap themselves around the bottom of the chairs,
Like a dragon has decorated the outside of his lair.

A cluster of bridesmaids, as pretty as can be,
All look so excited, from what I can see.
Some in a precious pink and some in baby blue,
Look like dissimilar flowers, which don't have a clue.

Suddenly the girls dash to the back of the hall,
To wait for the princess to arrive at the ball.
Whisper, whisper. Hush, hush,
Begins to ripple through the church, like the leaves on a bush.

Standing next to the altar, the handsome groom awaits his bride,
He is standing tall and bursting at the seams with pride.
Dressed all in black with his hair combed straight,
You can tell he is hoping and praying that the bride won't be late.

At long last a beautiful snow queen appears in the doorway,
Her long, flowing hair shines in the dazzling sun of the new day,
From somewhere in the church, a thunderous organ begins to play,
Here comes the bride, here comes the bride,
Family and friends are blasted away!

As the snow queen turns to face her king,
Her veil is unfolded from her face as swift as a dove's wing,
Will you be his wife? Will you be her husband?
The swapping of the rings lasts only for a second.

Hannah Thompson (13)
Archbishop Temple School

CHRISTMAS POEM

It's Christmas Day and everyone's merry,
The whole family's here to celebrate,
Grandma's sat in our blue armchair, drinking her glass of sherry,
Uncle John rushes through the door, all wrapped up from the cold,
The walls are all decorated with holly and berries.

Santa's been, his gifts of toys and games, covered with vibrant paper,
Lizzy's tearing at her presents just like a wild cat,
All the children are screaming and running around with Coke,
Making them hyper.
I open Grandma's gift; I guessed, a knitted scarf - as usual.
I wonder if she has a secret knitting workshop?
Grandad's probably her helper.
By the window is the tree sparkling with twinkling lights,
Standing tall and pretty.

Mum comes in with a plump roast turkey with all the trimmings,
Everyone shouts hooray at the sight of food,
We all sit at the table covered in tinsel and party hats,
The house is full of laughter on this Christmas Day
As everyone's in a happy mood,
After lunch the room hears sounds of moans and groans
When everyone's finished pud.

I look past the gleaming tree over to the panelled window,
At the falling snow,
It looks like fluffy cotton wool covering the ground,
Crunch! Under every footstep,
Then I seem to her a faint cry. 'Ho Ho Ho!'
Santa must be with his reindeer soaring through the sky.

Susan Rodger (14)
Archbishop Temple School

RED

What is red?
Red is a burning sunset
Above a deserted beach
With glistening waves lapping to and fro
Or could it be
A clown's nose,
A ruby
And a ripe strawberry?
A Red Admiral spreads its wings
To cool down on a summer's day
And red is a velvet cushion that the Queen's crown sits upon.
Red is
Passion
And rich red wine at Christmas
Red is
Illness,
Anger
Embarrassment.
The church bells boom and ring
And flowers blossom for the spring.
Red is a field full of poppies
Never-ending.

Laura Arpino (12)
Archbishop Temple School

THE SWING

Look at the leaves on the ground,
Listen to the crunching sound.
The trees are empty,
So are the streets.

Autumn's gone and winter's coming,
Imagine all the happy faces at Christmas.

Christmas is over and so is the new year,
But suddenly I hear a cheer.

Children everywhere in the snow,
But I know soon they'll have to go.
I'm on the swing, all alone,
All I can hear is that original swinging tone.

Adam Pourmahak (12)
Archbishop Temple School

CELEBRATION

Celebrations are such fun,
Playing games with everyone.
Birthdays, Christmas and Hallowe'en too,
Presents, decorations, nice and new.

Jelly, ice cream and chocolate cake,
Lots and lots of food to make.
Super salmon sandwiches and scrumptious sausage rolls,
Different flavoured crisps dozing in little fancy bowls.

Presents all of different sizes,
Each one holding big surprises.
Dressed in pretty paper with silky shiny bows,
All waiting silently in neat and tidy rows.

People dancing with games to play,
Everyone's having a fantastic day.
Party poppers popping, *pop! pop! pop!*
Disco music blasting out non-stop.

It's time to go, it's getting late,
We wave goodbye at the garden gate.
The party's ended like a bursting balloon,
We hope there will be another one soon!

Ruth Phillips (12)
Archbishop Temple School

CHRISTMAS POEM

The great big, green tree,
Stands there feeling lonely,
Everybody's drinking tea,
You can hear the children moaning.
The miles of tinsel glistening in the
lights for Christmas to be,
Makes many more people have delightful faces,
Not at all any groaning.
What a wonderful sight.

Big bows, big presents,
Small presents make everyone cheer.
Children laughing with much excitement
and all being merry,
Adults laughing, drinking the old sherry.
What a wonderful sight.

Carol singers merrily singing,
Many neighbours joining in.
Church bells in the distance ringing,
Calling people to go in.
In the street you can hear a jingling,
Must be the tunes at the Holiday Inn.
What a wonderful sight.
Christmas is such a happy time so come in
and join the fun.
Be quiet over the night,
so not even a mouse can cry.
Merry Christmas,
What a wonderful sight.

Emma Bamber (13)
Archbishop Temple School

SKIING

A sudden lurch as the lift sets off,
Crawling its way up the mountain.
Boulders and trees,
Mountains and moguls,
Mounds and jumps surround us.
Crawling our way up the mountain.

The doors open and we step out,
the wailing wind whips our ears and scratches our eyes.
We clip up our boots,
Tighten out coats,
And with a cry we ride off against the probing weather.
The wailing wind whips our ears and scratches our eyes.

We hit the powder,
Like flour in the blizzard.
Our edges dig deep,
Poles held high,
The skies have a life of their own.
The snow is like flour in the wind.

We come to a stop,
Gaze out into the chequered valley and beyond.
The light misty snow swirls around the land,
And roads like springs meander down hairy mountain backs.
The mountains themselves pierce the sky,
And the valleys delve deep into the bedrock.
The storm is upon us and we set out,
Gazing out into the valley chequered and beyond.

With the blizzard behind us and powder in front
We will be skiing well into the night!

Stuart Connolly (12)
Archbishop Temple School

SPRING IS HERE!

Spring is here! She is creeping upon us, awakening sleeping baby buds
into multicoloured suns that sway in the soft, warm breeze.
Spring makes a tiny drip of water into a gurgling stream that will now
make its way down the dry bed, passing the crowd of daffodils and then
finally to the dewy, green carpet where the infant lambs are
satisfied by its coming.

The sun is back! After its long, dark rest of autumn and winter,
the sun shows off, sending bright, white rays of sunlight
onto the re-leafed trees.
With green, oval, flat balls that cast a shadow on the aged, orange, dry
leaves lying in the shadow of the past, which is autumn and winter.

If spring is this beautiful, with blossoming trees, covered in pink
balls of cotton wool and little lambs prancing and playing games
in the field,
I can't wait until summer, can you?

Rachel St Clair Fisher (13)
Archbishop Temple School

MY CELEBRATION

Birthdays are a special treat,
One at which families like to meet,
Sharing presents, cards and fun,
The celebration has now begun.

There's a birthday cake,
That's freshly baked,
Candles increasing each year,
Each one bringing birthday cheer.

Presents are the very best part,
Each one given with a thought from the heart,
Presents, paper, gift tags too,
Sparkling, bright and shining new.

11 o'clock comes too soon,
Through the window we can see the moon,
Dad's car will soon be here,
The celebration is over until next year.

Lucy Crook (12)
Archbishop Temple School

RED

What is red?

Red is a volcano,
Red is a car,
Red is a postbox, I can see from afar.

Red can be anger,
Red can be a poppy,
Red can be confused from an exciting cliffhanger!

Red can be feelings all bottled up inside,
Red can be the embarrassment of a fall down a slide.
Red can be the sun glowing onto Earth,
Red can be the coldness of a Scottish town, Perth.

But the best thing to us about the colour red,
Is that all these ideas are our jumbled in our heads.

Carolyn Thompson & Louise Page (12)
Archbishop Temple School

BONFIRE NIGHT

Jumping up and down by the door,
Getting mud all over the floor.
So excited, I just can't wait,
Telling my dad, 'We're going to be late!'

Finally get there,
Now we're inside.
Get money from my dad
And go on the rides.

Go near the bonfire,
Finally warm.
Starting to feel hungry,
Buy some popcorn.

I buy a sparkler,
Give it a light.
I watch the sparks
Disappear into the night.

Up go the rockets,
Like spaceships in the sky.
Millions of colours,
People gasp, 'Oh my!'

Time to go home,
My mum wipes a tear.
I ask her, 'Why?'
She says, 'We will have to wait another year.'

Joshua Harper (12)
Archbishop Temple School

AUTUMN AND BONFIRE NIGHT

Autumn's in the air
Dew like diamonds on the ground.
Fallen leaves are everywhere,
Conkers to be found.

It's that time of year
The nights are drawing in
Bonfire Night's coming
Fantastic fireworks are in the tin.

The bonfire's lit
Potatoes are nearly done.
The hot dogs are cooking,
Let's start the fun.
Fountains pouring sparks,
Coloured lights in the black night sky,
Air bombs screeching,
Rockets fly.

The flames are dying,
The food's all gone.
The tin is empty,
The fireworks are done.

The excitement is over
For yet another year.
Sad children all go home,
But cheer up, Christmas will soon be here!

Matthew Heywood (12)
Archbishop Temple School

CHRISTMAS EVE

Christmas is the time I love,
It's wonderful, happy and jolly.
Baubles hang gently from the tree,
As well as mistletoe and holly.

I put the angel upon the tree,
Her wings are spread like she could fly.
To spread Christmas spirit about,
I stare at her way up high.

The presents are underneath the tree,
Some are long; others are wide.
They are all different shapes and sizes,
Most are brightly wrapped and tightly tied.

So hurry up Christmas,
I'll try to sleep.
But be quick
Before I begin to peep!

Jenny O'Connell (12)
Archbishop Temple School

PANDA

Panda is asleep on the ground,
He moves his paw and opens his eyes.
He gropes to see if bamboo is around,
Round here it looks like just bugs and flies.

Panda stretches, then he yawns,
Then he yelps and screams.
He notices he's in a patch of thorns,
He rolled over in the night it seems.

Panda tries to awake, he really tries,
He takes the weight off his paws.
He yawns again then closes his eyes,
It looks like he's asleep once more.

Alexandra Turner-Piper (12)
Archbishop Temple School

CHRISTMAS DAY

Outside my house carols are sung,
with children playing by their side,
each one was wrapped up warm.
The sweet children are all so young.

It gets darker, each curtain is shut
Off we go to our beds.
We were up in the morning full of joy,
what's in the living room? I'll go and look.

I sit around the Christmas tree,
the presents are all opened.
I love this time of year,
it's the best time for me.

The presents are now all there,
broken or in pieces.
My brother, naughty as he is,
is sat upon the stair.

The day is now over, we had lots of fun,
playing games and talking,
eating our dinner with our hats on.
Away go the presents we've been given or won.

Zoe Cross (13)
Archbishop Temple School

CELEBRATIONS

Presents, presents everywhere,
Should I open one, do I dare?

Carefree, committed chocolate cake,
The sweets are dancing on the candy dish,
All for us to eat.

People playing games, the music's booming,
And in I come zooming.
Now I am ready,
Let's open the presents,
I choose the biggest one,
It's as big as the tallest skyscraper.

I open one bit, two bits and one more
What is it I wonder?
Out jumps a teddy bear,
'Happy birthday!'
Everyone yells.

Bang! Crash! Wallop!
The party poppers go.
The giant bear is an elephant.

Today is my day,
Well, that's what my parents say.

My friends have gone,
I'm the only one,
It's time for bed,
Off I go with the memories, which will last forever.

Sian Worthy (12)
Archbishop Temple School

CHRISTMAS

It's nearly Christmas; I just can't wait!
With all the decorations up, the house is looking great!
We are really busy; there's a lot to be done,
But Christmas time is always fun.

Christmas time is just the best:
Time to enjoy, time also to rest.
Because there isn't any school,
There's two whole weeks with no work at all.

There's Christmas pud and Christmas cake
And lots of other things to make.
There are also other things to do,
But there are other people to help out too.

It's worth it all because on the day,
We know we'll get our well-earned pay:
Christmas presents for you and me,
Underneath the Christmas tree.

But that's not all that Christmas is:
Under the fuss and fun and fizz,
We need to think, to open our eyes
And see where the real meaning lies.

For Christmas is when our Saviour came,
Jesus Christ, the Messiah his name,
The Son of God, the Prince of Peace,
He came that evil ways might cease.

So when Christmas does begin,
Take some time to think of him.

Elizabeth Parsons (12)
Archbishop Temple School

A CELEBRATION OF NATURE

Spring

The daffodils dance out from the soil,
The rosebuds push out to a dark red royal,
Blossoms fall like balloons from the sky,
Floating down from so very high
Young new lambs prance in the sun,
All the animals having fun.

Summer

August showers cover the ground,
Raindrops fall without a sound.
Children playing in the pool,
Drinks with ice, nice and cool.
The sun dances in and out of a cloud.
A bird swoops down as if it has bowed.

Autumn

The wild wind whistles like the wail of a banshee,
The autumn leaves 'crunch' as if they're moaning at me.
Smash! Goes the conker as it loses the fight,
Old owl hoots at the stroke of midnight.
The hedgehog sleeps softly in hibernation.
Whoosh goes the snow and autumn is gone.

Winter

Pretty patterned snowflakes fall from the sky.
Children build a snowman and dress him in a tie.
Look out of the window and what do you see?
Children on the ice, skating with glee.
Winter's almost over, how do we know?
The snowdrop is a symbol of joyous winter's glow.

Elizabeth Snalam (12)
Archbishop Temple School

STAGGER THROUGH A GRAVEYARD

As I make my way in-between stony graves,
Skeletons entwine their bony branches
Making pictures of pure evil descending upon me,
Shards of grass like drawn daggers ready for the kill,
My heart thumps and rebounds through every centimetre of my body,
Whilst every breath, every millimetre of my lungs has sharp needles,
Seeping slowly through the cold metal stabbing into me.

I quicken my pace and drag my feet,
Feelings start to drown in my head and there is a blur all around,
'Help!' I scream.
It echoes in my head as I fall into the hands of God.
I woke and stared,
I cannot answer for my terrifying dream.
Why?

Joanna Tomsett (14)
Carr Hill High School

THE MUSE

'The Muse descends!'
She said, she lied,
The Muse has got stuck on a cloud,
I try and I sigh,
Inspiration runs dry,
Ideas all left in a crowd.

I put pen to paper,
Words begin to pour,
My Muse has escaped from the sky,
I glow and I flow
When my Muse makes a show
And I get on a poetry high!

Hazel Sumner (15)
Carr Hill High School

MY WORLD

From the roar of a dragon,
to the clash of a sword,
this is the story,
from my world.

Disaster, deception,
masters and kings,
these are not,
wonderful things,
in my world.

Gods and myths,
creatures of old,
dragons of elements,
brave and bold,
from my world.

They go through my head,
like a picture book,
as I gaze at the ceiling,
wondering what I'd be like,
without my world.

Tamara Astley (15)
Carr Hill High School

RIDER'S TIDE

Trapped between two forces,
Desire or duty? A dangerous choice,
Through the shadows, through the trees,
A deadly secret, fatal.
Heart of rage, heart of fear,
Bea, careless heart.
Yet another secret lies,
Border to border a raid they plan.

Cockleshell cross, over the sand,
Midnight silence, say nothing but 'goodbye'
Yet something feels . . . wrong,
The air shifts, the feeling builds,
Gut instinct? Or is it of heart, liver and brain?
The bright hazel eyes are wide and wild,
With an arching cry he somersaults,
Away, backwards . . . out of sight.

Alex Winter (13)
Carr Hill High School

LEAVING

I'm going now, leaving
You'll never see me again
Goodbye, ta-ta, au revoir,
Bye-bye.
However you say it
It all means the same
I'm leaving
I'll fly
Miles, hours
I'm there.
For the pain
I have caused you
Was so great
And now it is
Worse
And I never said
Sorry.

Stephen Sumner (13)
Carr Hill High School

I'M SAFE

The sun has gone down
The streets have gone dark
The street lamps are baring their yellow teeth
And the beast cars are zooming up and down.
I'm being chased by a gang of newspaper gremlins
Illuminated by the glow of the eager cat.
I've spotted the bus, I've got to get on.
I'm on, I'm safe
But wait, it's broken-down.
I can see the beady eyes of a monster car
It's heading towards us
Quick, I've got to get off.
I'm off and look, the sun has come up.
   I'm safe.

Paul Horrocks (11)
Christ The King RC High School

THE WINTER FOX

The strange fox steps into winter,
He steps into the snow like a splinter.
Soon the snow comes crashing down,
His frosty tail tries not to drown.
He quickly goes and hides behind a tree
And he wraps his tail around his knee.
Soon the snow dies away
And here comes another day.
Now the fox goes to his cave
And he hides in his grave for the next winter.

Shabana Moreea (12)
Christ The King RC High School

SS Paper

I built myself a spaceship
Out of paper and glue.
I filled the tank with orange juice
And flew to the moon.

I stopped there for my dinner
Then continued on to Mars.
Twice around Jupiter's rings
Refuelling at the stars.

Passing through the Milky Way
Now I'm going home.
Crash-landing in the garden
I broke Dad's gnome.

Deanna Schulz (11)
Christ The King RC High School

Friends

Are we friends or are we not?
You told me once and I forgot.
So tell me now and tell me true,
So I can say I'll be there for you.
From all the friends I've ever met,
You're the one I like the best.
And if I die before you do,
I'll go to Heaven and wait for you.
I'll give the angels back their wings,
And give the loss of everything,
Only to prove our friendship is true,
I'd like to say *I love you!*

Hafizah Mulla (15)
Christ The King RC High School

THUNDER

Hear the thunder
Hear the roar
See the rain
Outside my door.
Hear the rain
All wet and windy
We hear the rain
Falling down our chimney.
Rainstorms
Come once a year
With them they bring
Nothing but fear.
Fear of thunder
Fear of rain
I wish they'd go
Away again.

Daniel Hodson (14)
Christ The King RC High School

MY ROOM

I love
my room
It may be a mess
but I love my room
Pens, pencils on the floor
I can only just open my door
But I love my room
Bogeyman Fred under the bed
but he might be dead
But I love my room.

Anthony Cook (12)
Christ The King RC High School

THE LISTENERS

The listeners
Listened and heard what the old man said.
He heard a creak while he lay awake,
So ever so slowly he turned his head,
'Who's there?' he said, but to no reply,
And then he remembered it was a stormy night,
He had that night a most terrible fright.
He woke up the next morning, but not in his bed,
He didn't know where, but was definitely dead.
He was in the walls, he could hear things said,
He was now a listener like the others who died
In this house on a stormy night.

James Grime (12)
Christ The King RC High School

WHY?

Why don't you have a think
Why you don't like pink?
Why do you like cake?
Why are there things you can't make?
Why are some people poor
Or is it that rich people want more?
Why is there a disease called smallpox
And why is there an XBox?
Why can't we be in peace?
No more wars, please.
Why are there lots of fish
And only some on the dish?
I know lots of people are dying
And why are people smiling?

Mohamed Patel (12)
Christ The King RC High School

THE GREAT FIRE OF LONDON

As the blaze goes higher, the brains shout 'Fire!'
As the sounds get higher, the people get lower.
The fire-fighters can't tackle the fire, the fire burns higher.
The people climbing, falling, rushing and slipping,
All come down like a ton of bricks,
Pile up in a heap one upon another.
The houses come down like a mountain of feathers,
The wood is like some black sugar,
Piling up layer by layer.
The fire grows higher.
The fire-fighters with their trucks and cars
Try to take down this enormous fire but,
The fire is fighting back.
The hours and hours of hard working,
Out of breath people lie in their beds,
Minute by minute, second by second, hour by hour
after fighting The Great Fire of London.

Omar Bhayat (14)
Christ The King RC High School

ABOUT A RAINBOW

Rain and sun together make the rainbow grow.
Flying in the clouds see their colours shine in the sky.
Indigo and violet, bands of red and blue.
Now it's bold and bright, then it fades right from the sky
Like a bridge over a coloured ribbon.
Over the fields and the shops,
Over the houses and the hilltops.
Then the world will come to an end
And the rainbow will clear like a gold bridge.

Gina Howarth (14)
Christ The King RC High School

BIRTHDAYS

Birthdays come to everyone,
A long time to come, but soon gone.
We all have one every year,
Gifts we give to people who are dear.
As children it's exciting,
Hoping and wishing,
Their birthday will arrive soon.
As elders we dread
Another year gone.
Balloons, presents, cards and cakes,
That's what a birthday makes.
To receive these from those we love
Makes us fit in our family
Like a hand in a glove.

Dean Farnworth (14)
Christ The King RC High School

STATIONERY

I have a lot of stationery
It's all in my bedroom
closet.

I buy stationery all the time
With the money in my
pocket.

The only problem now is
I just can't get to
close it.

Tasneem Patel (12)
Christ The King RC High School

MY SISTER LAURA

My sister Laura
She is quite small
Although I love her
We sometimes brawl.

I easily get wound up
It's like she's my mum
She steals all my stuff
She thinks I'm dumb.

She has extensions in her hair
Long and silky brown
It takes her days to get it right
She always wears it down.

Whenever we argued
I always dissed her
But then went back and kissed her
Cos I love her, she's my sister.

Lisa Cooper (14)
Christ The King RC High School

SPORTS DAY

I love Sports Day,
It is an exciting day.
I always win
And at the end I always throw up in the bin.

I break some records
And people are videoing me.
Can you beat me?
I don't think so.

Abubaker Nakhuda
Christ The King RC High School

IT'S A DOG'S LIFE

Dogs just lie there on the floor,
Dogs just sit behind the kitchen door.
Dogs have it easy, dogs have it good,
Their favourite thing is to roll in mud.
Dogs sometimes scare you when they bark,
Especially when you're in the park.
Dogs like to chase after a ball,
Sometimes they bring it back when you call.
Dogs are all shapes, sizes and colours,
Some are slim, some are fuller.
Dogs don't have to go to school to learn,
Oh, I wish I could have a turn,
To stay in my bed all day
And dream the day away.

Kevin Hopwood (15)
Christ The King RC High School

GOING FOR A WALK

I like going for walks,
So with my friends I can talk.
Strolling through the grass
And all the huge trees we go past.
Sliding down the slide,
Then through the plants we glide.
Looking up at the sky,
We watch the birds go by.
I like going for walks,
So with my friends I can talk.

Hajara Patel (12)
Christ The King RC High School

LOVE

Love is like a golden stream
When I look at you I see a bright, white beam
Your eyes are like the stars above
Your face is like a flying dove
Your lips are like a clown's red nose
I really want to marry you but I don't know how to propose
Your heart is like a rose on fire
You are the one I desire
Take me now and never forget
I will always be your faithful pet
Hold my hand and look within
Now we can start afresh and begin
Be my bride and come with me
I've got a one-way ticket to eternity
Take this ring and think of me
As a man with a heart and a heart for thee.

Ryan Malik (15)
Christ The King RC High School

SCHOOL IS FUN

I like school better than home,
School is good, but not better than swimming,
School is fun but I like swimming,
All the time I want to come to school
And learn everything all the time
It is good learning all the time
School is great sometimes
I want to go home and play with my friends
And go back to school.

Neesha Hussain (11)
Christ The King RC High School

HAUNTED HOUSE

Far away, abandoned in the dark, stood a house.
I thought I would be brave, so I went to the spooky, dead house.
Behind me the door banged shut, then out of the blue
                              the telephone rang.
I picked it up and someone said, 'Get out while you can.'
I went upstairs and heard a squeak, I thought it was a creak,
Saw a mouse and I screamed out the house and never went there again.

Stephanie Gibson (13)
Christ The King RC High School

FOOTBALL

F   ootball is the best sport.
O   ther people don't like football.
O   pen-air games are good for you.
T   en a-side on the pitch.
B   alls are coming side to side.
A   ny person can try football.
L   et's try and get into the league.
L   ast week we won the game.

Wessley Riding (12)
Christ The King RC High School

THE POND

The pond down the lane,
Children use it like a drain.
Oil from the road is washed in,
Killing all the fish, frogs and toads.

Steven Hills (14)
Christ The King RC High School

MY POEM JUST FOR YOU

I may not be any good at maths,
But I've been counting the minutes up since you have been gone,
And it's 450.
I may not be any good at geography,
But I know when you're at the other end of the world.
I may not be any good at history,
But I can remember the good times we had.
I may not be any good at English,
But I sure know how to write to you.
I may not be any good at Spanish,
But I would learn it for you.
I may not be any good at science,
But I can easily say that *our* love is an element of love.
I may not be any good at art,
But I can sure picture what you look like.
I may not be any good at PE,
But I would run a mile just to see you.
I may not be any good at romance,
But my heart is telling me to love.
I may not be any good at shopping,
But I would buy you the world if I could.
I may not be any good at making friends,
But when we're together we wouldn't need any.
I may not be any good at driving,
But I would crash into everything just to be with you.
I may not be any good at music,
But for you I would play only the sweetest melodies.
I may not be any good at anything in this world,
But for you I would . . . *do everything!*

Alan Parker (15)
Christ The King RC High School

SEA CREATURES

As the pale people of Blackpool
Turn into scarlet rows,
They are oblivious to the monster
That wets and licks their toes.

This monster is a wild beast
With the strength and power of thunder
And the monster has a giant jaw
Which eats boats to feed its hunger.

But the monster is a unicorn
With a silver, silky mane,
Which pushes waves upon the rocks
To make glistening, sparkling rain.

Richard J Lonsdale (13)
Garstang High School

CHANGING TIDES

The blue, everlasting sea's beautiful and calm first thing,
Stretching further than my eyes can see,
The moon so powerful it can control the tides.

The sea's rough and tough,
changing, turning, churning upside down,
crashing, bashing against the cliffs' sides.

It's quiet and calm,
lonely, but charmed,
reflections deep as the sun goes down.

Tomorrow it begins again.

Lauren Harrison (13)
Garstang High School

THE HARSH SEA

The sea smashes into the rocks,
To men it still intrigues and shocks,
It wears down all that it touches,
It tries to break all that it clutches,
It rolls onto beaches,
It howls and it screeches.

The sea is cruel and cold,
It snatches for things to twist and hold,
It sinks a ship like a toy,
The ship goes down like an innocent boy,
The crew helpless go down and down,
In the depths they tumble and drown.

The sea is but an ancient machine,
Its waves are blue and its plants are green,
It can be as harsh as an angry teacher,
But its signature resembles a creature's,
Its waves can be as high as hills,
In sailors their fear of it still distils,
For its power is above all that thrills.

Dickon Whitewood (13)
Garstang High School

THE SEA

The sea is a lion standing tall and proud,
He lifts his lumbering head to see all in front
And bellows out a roar strong and loud.
He runs forward towards his prey
And pounces, crashing down with immense force.
He returns home, there to stay,
He will attack again another day.

Alex Taylor (13)
Garstang High School

THE SEA

You can hear the sea for miles as the loud
Crashing waves, smack against the jagged
Rocks.
People scream when they hear the waves
Roar as they tumble on the beach shore.
Children's footprints get destroyed as the
Sea covers them up like a new, blue bed
Sheet.
Sandcastles get obliterated by the big,
Deep, dark sea.
Crabs and insects run for their lives as the
Ocean swallows them up, with one big gulp.
Seagulls glide low looking for food but
Without knowing the dangers of the sea.
In a couple of minutes the sky is empty, the
Beach is unoccupied, the sea is roaring
With victory.

Joe Miller
Garstang High School

THE SEASIDE SMELL

The smell of sea water calms my nose
The smell of the seaside.
The smell of boat fuel ruins the place
The smell of the seaside.
The smell of a morning beach is so lovely
The smell of the seaside.
The smell of suntan lotion
The smell of the seaside.
The smell of seaweed
The smell of the seaside.

Matthew Jepson
Garstang High School

THE SEASONS OF THE SEA

The sea in the spring
The sea when you can hear it sing
The feet in the sand
As the boats come to land.

The sea in the summer
The sea when you can hear the birds murmur
The shells get washed away by the waves
And they splash into the caves.

The sea in the autumn
The sea when the sea creatures slither along the bottom
They swim and splash
And the rocks and water crash.

The sea in the winter
The sea when you see it glitter
The wind howls and blows
And everyone is dressed in warm winter clothes.

Hannah Prest (12)
Garstang High School

THE SEA

On the still, hot summer days,
The sea sends in her gentle waves,
Lapping silently upon the shore,
While the gulls above do soar.

When the high spring tides arrive,
Their waves reach up to the sky,
Their crests provide a silver way,
For surfers to skim around the bay.

In winter the storm winds blow,
The high-crested waves come crashing to the shore,
Wreaking havoc on the beach,
Depositing shells and pebbles by the score.

When gentle breezes blow,
Small boats sway to and fro,
Amongst the wispy, rippled sea,
The sailors come home for their tea.

Claire Howell (12)
Garstang High School

THE SEA

The sea, the sea, the sea
   Is as dark as night
The sea, the sea, the sea
   Is wild like a lion

The sea, the sea, the sea
   Is like a lion biting the stone
The sea, the sea, the sea
   Is a machine going in and out

The sea, the sea, the sea
   Is a boat
The sea, the sea, the sea
   Which carries boats along

The sea, the sea, the sea
   Whines like a child
The sea, the sea, the sea
   And just the sea.

Jessica Kershaw (12)
Garstang High School

THE CRASHING WAVE

Over the waves I go,
It's like swimming in snow,
It's so peaceful here.

Oh no! What's that I hear?
A gigantic wave like a tonne of bricks
Crashes down on me
And down and down I go,
Under the sea I try to stare
Trying to get a breath of air,
Swimming and swimming I try to swim high,
Words in my mind say, you're going to die.
I listen and listen, I hear a cry
It sounds like a dolphin nearby.
It's coming, it's coming really close
My mind blacks out.
By morning I'm on the coast.

James Eaton
Garstang High School

THE SEA

The crash of waves, white horses on
The beach.
Ridges in the sand, coves and bays,
Lighthouses that flash their signals
To the ships, protecting them from the
Rocks and shoals.
From grey to green, the sea shows many
Colours, many moods
As it rises and falls with the tides.

Stephen Rogers (14)
Garstang High School

MEDITERRANEAN SEA

M agical water
E ver so clear
D arting fish
I n and out
T ropical rainbows
E ver so bright
R ushing water
R unning near
A fter the sun
N ight-time comes
E ver so peaceful
A nd quiet and still
N ever to disturb

S o tranquil
E verything resting
A nd the water's still.

Jennifer Ball (12)
Garstang High School

THE SEA

As I walked to the rough sea,
The waves crashed into the rugged rocks,
I could smell the slimy seaweed,
Sharp shell lay on the beach
like people sunbathing,
Dead jellyfish lay on the sandy shore,
Cool breezes came from the cold, salty sea,
Boats came in from the dark blue sea like a fleet of planes,
And then slowly but surely, the tide came in
Like a fan was blowing it in.

Adam Roskell
Garstang High School

THE SEA

Listen to the sea,
Smashing,
Bashing,
Crashing against the rocks.

Listen to the sea,
Making ripples in the sand,
Swishing,
Swirling,
Going out to sea.

I like to watch the sea,
I give it a wave
And it waves back.
It goes
Swishing,
Swirling,
All the way back.

Tracey Dainty (12)
Garstang High School

UNTITLED

In the sea it is like a king ruling everywhere
Eating away at the rock.

Boats trying to survive
In the clashing waves.

People trying to keep it steady
Stopping it from going.

But soon they just can't handle it
Then it's at the bottom of the sea.

David Kelsall
Garstang High School

THE SEA

The sea is a boisterous beast,
The waves crashing on the rocks,
The sea like a piece of blue, silk material
The salty smell and taste is bitter.

The sun reflects on it like a mirror,
The sand a wet, golden carpet,
The creatures swimming about hunting for food.

Lastly, as the sun sets, the sea turns
A sparkly silver, star-like,
The sea is now a sleeping baby,
Creatures all settled.

Gillian Eakhurst (13)
Garstang High School

THE SEA

The sea has loads of secrets,
Very little of them told.
Although the sea is ancient,
When new ones are found, it's gold.

The sea has different features,
The waves, the salt, the sand.
And when the waves come rolling in,
It's like a waving hand.

As night-time falls, the sea is calm
And piles of sand are flattened.
The last person walks off the beach,
As though the sea's forgotten.

David Wood (13)
Garstang High School

THE SEA

The sun shines down on the sea
The dark green, blues of the sea,
The clear, deep waters look crystallized
When calm and peaceful.

But then the wind blows a gale
And waves begin to appear,
The waves then crash on the shore
The sea coming in near and near.

But then the sun's rays
Shine through the darkened clouds
And the sea is back to normal,
For now.

Laura Tattersall (12)
Garstang High School

THE TIDE

The flowing of the tide,
Peaceful, gentle, smooth.
Streaming through the open sea,
Silent as the moon.

Creeping with a little sound,
Climbing up the bay.
Rippling, expanding,
Smoothing out the sand.

The little sound has grown,
Replaced with louder noise.
It passes from the quiet,
With a mighty surge of spray.

Esther Cornall (12)
Garstang High School

MY SEA HORSES

My beautiful, pearly-white sea horses race to greet me,
I stand there watching them licking my feet
And then to all the herd grazing as calm as a
Starry sky.

Most of the time they let surfers ride on them
And children play among them.
Some people do not care for my horses,
They poison them with oil and petrol.

My horses are going out now,
But they will come back to greet me again.
Tomorrow I hope,
So I can gaze upon them and marvel at my sea horses.

Megan Tudor (12)
Garstang High School

THE SEA

The sea is like a never-ending puddle,
deep and blue, wide and big.
The waves are like a racing horse
bold and white, big and strong.

The fish are like colourful collages,
shiny and slippery, small and fast.
The sea horses are like the horses on a carousel,
swift and small, sleek and colourful.

The sand is like the grains of time waiting to be counted
yellow and grainy, bright and full.
The pebbles are like grey curled up cats,
grey and solid, big and small.

Ashleigh Jenkinson (12)
Garstang High School

THE SEA

The sea is a raging monster
He tosses and turns all day
In and out
He swishes about
Changing the beach each day.

Splash! Crash! Bang!

The sea is a fluttering butterfly
He waves at us every day
Although he can swell
We see all is well
Under the sea today.

Splish! Splash! Spray!

Emma Wherry
Garstang High School

THE SEA

The sea is blue,
the sand is the colour of the sun on a cloudless day,
the sky is like a beautiful day in May,
the seagulls squawk for their dinner
because the time is coming very near.

The creatures in the bottom of the sea
potter around making a kind of squawky sound,
the sun is about to set,
everybody has had fun
now everybody is packing away
to wait for another day.

Katie Parkinson (13)
Garstang High School

THE LIGHT BLUE SEA

The dark, deep, destroying sea crashes into the rocks
like a hammer into a nail.
There are lots of fish shimmering
like a silver ring in the sun.
There is a mermaid in the distance
laughing and smiling.
A humungous whale jumps over her while flipping round
like lots of Waltzers flashing.
I get hit by a wave, it is warm and fuzzy
like a hot, woolly jumper on a winter's day.
I fall in the water so refreshing
I stay there all day.

Alex Barnett (14)
Garstang High School

WHIRLING WAVES

Whirling waves splash
against my face,
As I jump into
the deep blue sea.
I swim to the bottom
like a speedy fish,
It's cold and lifeless
like being in space.
As I swim to the top,
I climb back into
my little blue boat.

Becky McGuire (14)
Garstang High School

THE SEA HORSE

The sea is like a galloping horse
Because it has no course
No north, no west, no south, no east
As it enjoys its massive feast
Of sand and rocks
Like when the horse head cocks
But as the horse runs off its socks
The sea just chews up the rocks
Rocks, rocks, rocks.

Scott Eccleston (12)
Garstang High School

PETS

I have a cat,
He loves to try to eat my pet rat,
He also sleeps on the back door mat.

I have a dog,
He is called Mog,
When he is asleep he looks like a log.

I have a rat,
Who is scared of the cat,
She is also scared of our other pet bat.

I have a bat,
Who gets on with the cat,
But he hates the rat.

I have an owl,
Who makes a big howl,
He hates the man on TV, Simon Cowell.

Lyndsey Amriding (12)
Our Lady's Catholic High School

MY BOXER

My boxer has fists like footballs,
He'll knock you out in one punch,
He doesn't like cats
But he does like his lunch.

He chases after butterflies
And gets stung by bees,
Hates the sound of music
But loves the sound of keys.

He's not like other boxers
Because he chases frogs,
He loves going for walks
Because he is a dog.

Elliot Ward (12)
Our Lady's Catholic High School

CATS

My feline friend by day
by night a hunter after prey,
soft fur and gentle paws,
watchful eyes and sharp claws,
a silent walk, a deadly stalk,
eyes that glint green,
a victim unknown seen,
whiskers twitch, an arching back,
an amazing leap and successful attack,
a limp corpse,
no remorse,
my cat I know,
but friend or foe?

Orla Norton (12)
Our Lady's Catholic High School

PASTA WITH CHICKEN SAUCE

Although the recipe sounds simple
And really tasty too
It's not as simple as it seems
There's a lot of work to do.

First you buy some pasta
Cream and fresh chicken too
Throw the chicken in a pan
And cook till 10 to 2.

Add some cream in your chicken
Put some pasta in your pan
Give everything a great good shake
Go pop open a nice cold can.

When you come back
You will see everything nearly done
All that needs doing now is serving in your mouth
And enjoy it, have some fun.

Rebecca Whitehead (12)
Our Lady's Catholic High School

MY MONKEY

In the jungle, he swings from tree to tree,
His eyes are like x-rays, searching for food.
When he finds it, he screeches like car brakes,
Then he hides, quiet as a mouse, eating,
Then he returns to the others
And later he sleeps.
My monkey,
Quiet and calm.

Emily Walker (12)
Our Lady's Catholic High School

MY PET RABBIT

Long, grey, floppy ears
Like long drooping curtains.
Hopping around the garden,
Like a frog in a pond!
Munching on her cabbage
Loud and clear.
Sleeping sweetly
Like a dove,
In her nest of hay!
Her long, soft, white fur
Squeaking for more food.
I just can't resist
That small sweet face!
Hiding in the hutch,
Under waterproof shelter.
Standing on her back 2 feet,
Just like the lion king!
What a perfect pet
My rabbit is!

Leanne Hartwell (12)
Our Lady's Catholic High School

THE WINDY WORLD

In the windy world it was so cold.
Trees rustled in the wind.
You can hear the noisy people
And the clock chimes in the steeple.
You can hear the fire burning
And the windy world turning.
You can feel the wind through the door
I don't want wind anymore.

Faye Smith (11)
Our Lady's Catholic High School

SNAKE

One fine day in the meadow,
I collected a bright green egg.
By accident I dropped it
And it shattered into bits,
My mum told me it was a snake,
An animal I loved to hate.

The next day I saw something,
That made my heart bleed.
A small snake, in my room,
I was sure I was doomed.

My dad came in and hit the snake,
It slithered on the floor,
One more swipe, it hit the door,
I was so scared, unprepared.

That day I was so lucky,
I felt smaller than a ducky.
I was scared, from that dreaded day
Until I was 20,
My birthday, today.

Luke Edelston (12)
Our Lady's Catholic High School

CHRISTMAS

I like Christmas, the cold and wintry nights,
I like Christmas, the trees and the lights,
I like Christmas, the writing and the wrapping,
I like Christmas, the snow and the bows,
I like Christmas, the gloves and hugs,
I like Christmas, the peas and the pudding.

Liam Bartlett (11)
Our Lady's Catholic High School

A CAT

Silent footsteps,
Like a professional spy,
Hunting its prey,
Mice and small birds, a feast
Hiding in bushes,
Like a shadow in the dark,
Under trees,
On rooftops,
Nowhere is out of bounds.
A soft purring noise,
Like a small car engine,
As a quick thank you,
Or a small squeak for attention
A human knee,
Is the perfect nest
On top of a cupboard
Or under a bed.

Elizabeth Atherton (12)
Our Lady's Catholic High School

KITTEN

She's grey and white, a tiny ball of fluff.
As dainty as a dancer as she runs and leaps,
Curls up, purring, on your knee to sleep.
Explores the garage, pounces and leaps.
As pretty as a picture as she peeps out from under the bed.
Miaows when she's hungry, gobbles up her food,
Licks herself clean, she's as smooth as silk.
Bounds away to play with her toys,
As mad as a hatter,
A kitten!

Elizabeth Rawcliffe (12)
Our Lady's Catholic High School

CICHLID

The cichlid is hungry,
Hungry for blood,
It needs to kill to survive.

A foolish fish enters the cichlid's territory,
Now is the time to strike,
The cichlid's eyes turn red with anger.

It dives out from the seaweed,
Taking down and killing its prey,
Like a ruthless demon.

The cichlid returns to the seaweed
Waiting to pounce,
Waiting for another catch.

Anthony Smith (12)
Our Lady's Catholic High School

CAT

Elegantly she strolls along,
Sly as a fox she plots,
Mice beware, here she comes,
Ready to pounce, crouched to the ground.

A shadow in the night,
Eyes like glass in the moonlight,
Pretty as a picture when morning comes,
Champion sweet-talker with purrs.

Ravenously she chews and drinks,
Proud as a peacock she boasts,
Her head up high as she strolls along,
Finally she falls asleep.

Zoe Sherrington (12)
Our Lady's Catholic High School

TUNA

The tuna
deadly sharp teeth
lined in their hundreds,
a natural born killing machine,
powerful but yet silent.
It waits for an unsuspecting fish
to come swimming by,
swimming right into the jaws of the tuna.
Once it has been fed it returns to the deep,
to wait, waiting for a long time,
waiting for another catch.

Faster than a bullet,
but yet very graceful.
Sometimes it comes to the surface to feed,
that is when the fishermen strike
and that is the end of a tuna's life.

Andrew Walsh (12)
Our Lady's Catholic High School

WHAT'S THAT?

What's that behind the door?
What's that upon the floor?
There's something all over the place
What's that, that flew across my face?

The scariest place I've ever been
The scariest place I've ever seen
What's that in my bed?
What's that on my head?
I desperately want to scream
But find out it's all a dream!

Stephanie Monks (11)
Our Lady's Catholic High School

THE KID

In primary school, he was a terror, never a kid,
Who was under the weather.

Liked to do things that were sometimes daunting,
Other times, very naughty.

He climbed trees and acted like cats,
But then fell out, he looked like a prat.

He stole library books and liked all the girls,
Used to smoke and hang out in loos.

He punched, pained, prodded, deafened, defeated
And dyed . . . (his hair).

Liked to lie, loot, hit, hide and fight,
Thought he was cool, but turned out not.

David Mortimer (14)
Our Lady's Catholic High School

THE ROLLER COASTER

As I went up the track
My stomach went tight
And when I reached the top
My mouth opened wide,
Then suddenly I tilted
And I then screamed throughout the ride.
In and out the loop the loops
And up and down the hills and bumps.
When I got off
I lined up again
And went on time after time.

Rachel Muncaster (11)
Our Lady's Catholic High School

AN OLD FRIEND

I have a friend, who I have not seen in years,
He was kind, caring, friendly, clever, funny, forgiving,
Tidy and sometimes very annoying.
He was good at maths, science and everything else apart from sport.
He could be popular one minute and be unpopular the next,
He got into lots of arguments and often got people into trouble,
He was popular with teachers and did what he was told.
He was like a teacher's pet and we took the mickey.
He was rejected by some and he was often pushed down the hill,
He was deliberately fouled at football
And he broke his foot in first year and we all laughed at him.
It was a bit tight really because we played lots of tricks on him,
But we all thought he deserved it because he was often too cocky.

Michael Weaver (14)
Our Lady's Catholic High School

TROPICAL FISH

Tropical fish swimming gently
Around the coral reef
It hides amongst the shells
Quiet as a kitten
It hears danger and darts
As fast as a bullet
It hides behind the rocks
So predators can't see it
Its beautiful rainbow tail follows
As it cautiously swims away
Searching amongst the seaweed for lunch
Finally it settles again
Under the calm blue sea.

Laura Gunson (12)
Our Lady's Catholic High School

STINGRAY

It glides through water,
like a plane in the air,
its tail floats behind it with that deadly sting
under rocks, over rocks, it can go almost anywhere.

The stingray lies on the seabed,
waiting for its prey,
it lies there so quiet, quiet as a mouse,
it waits, and waits, and waits, and waits,
then when the time is right
it strikes, and it strikes with that deadly sting.

This fish won't go hungry.

Tom Sweeney (12)
Our Lady's Catholic High School

THE SHARK

He swims deep in the ocean
Never seen out in the open
Lurking in the darkness
Ready to strike.

He sinks small ships
And he's extremely fierce
He bites his food with a deadly pierce
He's a swift swimmer
With a pointed fin.

Watch out he's coming
Swim, swim, swim!

Matthew Blackburn (11)
Our Lady's Catholic High School

IN MY MIND I SEE . . .

In my mind I see what
my perfect world would be.

Children playing all day long
the choir singing their favourite song.

Bands playing soothing music
as people lie there listening.

Adults lazing,
the sheep grazing.

Children playing, having fun,
as adults lie there under the sun.

Now the day is ending
and the sun is setting,
everyone goes in
for their good night's rest.

Hope Coupe (11)
Our Lady's Catholic High School

GOLDFISH

How it moves like a tortoise
And as quick as lightning,
It hides in a treasure chest,
If scared it will not hesitate.

It sucks the food in,
Into its mouth,
It sleeps silently
And close to the top.

Joseph Colledge (12)
Our Lady's Catholic High School

BOLD EAGLE

It waits like a female lion hunting its food,
It's peaceful like a baby as it snoozes off to dreamland,
As it flies over mountains and rivers,
It snaps at the chance to catch its delicious dinner,
It flies like an elegant swan,
With his shiny yellow beak and eyes shining
As he's soaring through the air like Concorde
Trying to take down other eagles like a tornado.

Christopher Shorrock (12)
Our Lady's Catholic High School

HAWKEYE

He flies around,
feathers as long as a rainbow,
eyes as sharp as a knife,
swiftly he moves as he watches his prey,
claws like daggers all through the day,
a high-pitched screech is the noise it makes,
moving through trees and over the lakes,
it talks to its friend with a caw.
What is it?
It's a *hawk!*

Heather Coulton (12)
Our Lady's Catholic High School

DAVID BECKHAM

My favourite player is David Becks,
Because he is fit, tanned and doesn't wear specks,
He plays for Man United and he is cool,
I wish he would play football with me at my school.

Everyone loves him from Manchester
To London, Essex to Peckham
Because is the England captain,
David Beckham.

Hayley Ryan (12)
Our Lady's Catholic High School

ELEPHANT

Moves like thunder pounding towards you,
Moves as quickly as a cheetah running for its prey,
Works like a bulldozer
As he pulls logs along the dirty floor,
As greedy as a monkey eating bananas,
Like a boy who is very hungry,
Like a baby eating,
As a pig rolling in the mud,
Sleeps as still as a chair,
Sleeps like a table.

Ashley Smith (12)
Our Lady's Catholic High School

SUSIE

My cat is very dear to me
But I'm always told to leave her be.
I love to play with her all day
Because she's so cute
And is never on mute.
She's so loud and I'm so proud
And have you heard?
She's just killed a bird!

Victoria Pearce (11)
Our Lady's Catholic High School

WINTER'S MOUTH

Winter draws in near
The leaves begin to fall
The sky becomes icy but clear
Jack Frost comes to call.

As the snow begins to drop
Like petals from the sky
The farmers bring in their crops
Summer birds need to fly.

Far away somewhere warm
They migrate towards the south
To hide from the winter storm
From winter's freezing mouth.

Winter's over now,
Spring will soon arrive,
Farmers prepare the plough -
Everything's alive.

Harry Hudson (11)
Our Lady's Catholic High School

ROBIN

Little robin finding food,
Amongst the snow and frost,
All alone without her mum,
She realises she's lost.

Little robin home at last,
Inside her cosy nest,
Protected from the freezing rain,
So she can sleep and rest.

Shazia Khan (12)
Our Lady's Catholic High School

A FOOTBALL POEM

Football is cool
We play it at school.
It can get mean
When you play for a team.
When we won the cup
We had a lot to sup!

Watching my team is fun,
Especially when you know they have won.
My favourite is Man U
But I like PNE too.

The World Cup is exciting
When England got through it was frightening.
I thought we'd win till
We lost to Brazil.
We need to win again,
Let's cheer on our men.

Thomas McCarthy (11)
Our Lady's Catholic High School

MY DOG

My dog is really cute,
She is always lazing around.
She lies in the sun
And gazes at the clouds.

She's soft and warm
And likes to play.
She fetches a ball
And barks a lot.

Helen Sykes (11)
Our Lady's Catholic High School

IN MEMORY OF OUR HEROES - WORLD WAR I

Streets are filled with people jumping up and down,
alleys and walkways of the town,
the atmosphere was happy and loud,
as soldiers waved so very proud,
they would fight and win the war,
in soldiers' minds that's what they saw,
war will be quick, with no fear at all,
advancing armies will just fall.

Training was easy, not very hard,
saluting the leader that was in charge,
some people suspected something was going wrong,
the weapons on show looked very strong,
but they just looked forward to what was coming their way,
believing everything leaders say,
soldiers charge at targets so still,
but no one knew if that would kill.

As they sat in dirt and mud,
waiting, bored in trenches dug,
they realise war is a mistake,
with no celebrations for them to make,
food was little and very bad,
soldiers waited with faces so sad,
beginning to miss loved ones at home,
the kids, the wives, left all alone.

Signals are given for soldiers to fight,
plucking up courage and all of their might,
thousands of men march 'over the top',
many die before you could say 'pop,'
slaughtered men look up with a glare,
they had no time to stand and stare,
'no-man's-land' was just a huge grave,
for soldiers injured they just couldn't save.

Army leaders were very mean,
to the trenches they will have never been,
stationed in houses comfy and big,
eating great meals like roast beef and pig,
the telephone was the only link they had to war,
what it was really like they never saw,
generals didn't have a clue what it was like,
to them it was as easy as riding a bike.

Films were shown to make soldiers fight,
films that were so mean they'd turn anyone white,
they showed the enemies beating mothers and children,
this made soldiers motivated to kill them,
of course this information was not true,
it's just one-sided information made to fool.

At the beginning a great adventure was afoot,
little did they know it would be devilishly hot,
nine million men's lives were taken,
many other men's minds were shaken,
on the most memorable day, the 11th of November,
the Germans decided to surrender,
the British, French and Americans won,
the war had ended from there on,
all promises made were never fulfilled,
just millions of soldiers savagely killed,
gravestones stretched as far as the eye could see,
surviving soldiers went home for tea,
in fields of poppies dead soldiers lay,
waiting for that very day,
when they will meet with kith and kin,
up there in Heaven, once again.

Lauren Birkenhead (14)
Our Lady's Catholic High School

WHAT I LIKE AND DISLIKE

I don't like cabbage
It makes me quiver,
I hate spiders
They make me shiver,
I don't like boys
They always moan,
I dislike teachers
They always groan.

I like music
But only a bit,
I love David Beckham
He is so fit,
I like playing football
But people take the mick.
I like being me.

Ashleigh Ryan (11)
Our Lady's Catholic High School

FOOD

Garlic bread for starters
Sunday roast for main course
For afters black sticky pudding,
With raisins and honey in a rich sauce.
Rice pudding with jam, yum, yum, yum,
Followed by chocolate for my tum.

Bread, butter and cheese
Is all I need to please
Rice, chicken and curry
Is perfect in a hurry.

James Green (11)
Our Lady's Catholic High School

CATS

Black cats,
Brown cats,
Grey, ginger, white.

Fluffy cats,
Scraggy cats,
What a happy sight.

Fat cats,
Thin cats,
All a delight.

Quiet cats,
Noisy cats,
Alley cats at night.

Young cats,
Old cats,
All very cute.

Black cats,
Brown cats,
Mixed colours too.

Sophie Greer (11)
Our Lady's Catholic High School

OCTOPUS

Head like a big balloon,
Tentacles like roots from a tree,
Eats like a hoover,
Sprays ink like a gun shoots bullets,
The ink paralyses like the venom of a snake,
It moves like a propeller.

James Bolton (12)
Our Lady's Catholic High School

TRUE COLOURS

I remember the first time we met,
The sun was shining,
The sky was blue,
All I had on my mind was you.

I remember the second time we met,
The night was cold,
You held me tight,
All my attention was on your sight.

I remember the third time we met,
We were all alone,
You said you loved me,
I thought we were meant to be.

I remember the fourth time we met,
It was raining and cold,
You seemed to be downhearted,
You told me we had to be parted.

I remember the fifth time we met,
We had the argument,
You raised your hand
And tried to send me to the promised land.

Now I see your true colours.

Jade Fowler (15)
Our Lady's Catholic High School

WARS

Lying here in my bed,
Listening to what was being said,
Oh where was my mother being led?
Families crouching in a shed,
Waiting for a bomb to land on their heads.

Soldiers walking through the streets,
Shooting anyone they happen to meet,
I wish I was home, safe and warm,
Instead of being cold and all alone.

Lauren Canavan (14)
Our Lady's Catholic High School

SHADOWS

At night when I'm alone,
When the world is sleeping,
I dream of mysterious, eerie creatures,
Shadow monsters.

Darkness looms around corners,
Shadow monsters appear,
From the blood-thick, black,
Starry night.

Moon glaring from inky sky,
Shadow monsters creep
Into empty, silent spaces,
To wait.

Rising sun wakes the world,
Shadow monsters scutter,
To a realm of cold, dark life,
To live.

I awake from dreams of darkness,
To a world of warm light,
Shadow creatures destroyed,
Until tonight.

Grace Fitzpatrick (11)
Our Lady's Catholic High School

IT'S THE BOX AND IT REALLY ROCKS!

It's fun to watch, it's on night and day,
But to watch it, you'll have to pay,
It's for the adults and for any old kid,
It's the best thing you bought or anyone did,
It's the box and it really rocks!

You can get extra channels, there are loads,
There are different programmes, from singing to toads,
From foods to adverts, from news to 'toons,
Makeovers to make-up, computers to moons,
It's the box and it really rocks!

The satellite's up, the video's in,
Put the volume up and make the lights dim,
Sit back and relax and watch the show,
Lie back on the sofa, you'll never want to go,
It's the box and it really rocks!

Ewan Miller (11)
Our Lady's Catholic High School

KAISER (THE DOG)

He walks to and fro in front of the window
Like a lion watching his prey.
He sleeps like a log all through the night
And stays awake during the day.
He is as quick as a cheetah when he chases his ball,
When he stands on two feet he can be very tall.
He pulls in front of everyone like a zoo animal trying to escape.
His tongue is as long as a roll of tape.
I play with him like any other friend
He's my dog Kaiser and this is the end.

Jason Machin (12)
Our Lady's Catholic High School

FAME!

I have a dream . . .
Something to strive for, some focus and some promise.
Fame is a lifelong dream of mine,
To have a job I would simply adore
Would be a dream come true.
To live the life most people want,
The glitz, the glamour, the showbiz.
But what would it really be like?
Your privacy would be stripped away,
There would be nowhere to run or hide.
Could I live like that?
No way, I crave privacy and never want to lose it.
I want to live a carefree life, free from worry and hassle
But could this really happen if I experienced fame?
The dream - the lights, the camera, the action.
The nightmare - no freedom, no life, no future.
How can I possibly choose?

Charlotte Davis (14)
Our Lady's Catholic High School

FOOD, BEAUTIFUL FOOD

A bacon butty's what I eat,
It is so nice, that fatty meat.
It goes down lovely with brown sauce,
So now bring on my second course.
My second course is tea and toast
And now I go to school and boast.
I get detentions quite a lot,
Because of this I'm not a swot.
But I'll tell you what's a real winner,
The time 12.30 and my school dinner.

Kyle Healy (11)
Our Lady's Catholic High School

WAR

What's the point in war and death,
when tears and pain is all that's left.
The broken buildings and dead streets,
war and terror is all that meets.
What's the point when in the end
you make an enemy and lose a friend.
Funerals and memorials - memories and pain,
as families and friends think of it again.
Another selfish attack to add to the list,
regardless of the people that will be missed.
What's the point - it brings more war here,
people live in revenge, others live in fear.
You don't know peace - until you know suffering.
You can fix damage but can't stop remembering.
Death, tears, hate, revenge and blood,
what's the reason - it's all misunderstood.
You can't replace lives, once they've gone, they've gone,
you can only say sorry, but what's done is done.

Sam Monks (14)
Our Lady's Catholic High School

PIZZAS

Of all the pizzas I have tasted,
None of which, I have wasted.
Pepperoni and ham are what I like best,
But I'm always keen to try the rest.
Salami and chicken and any other meat,
But all the vegetables I will not eat.
Pizzas are my favourite food,
If I don't get pizzas I'm in a mood.

Damian East (11)
Our Lady's Catholic High School

ALONE

I am alone
So very alone

I am hurt
So very bad

I am ignored
Just thrown aside

I am security
For others to have

I am lonely
There is no one close
No one sees the pain

I cry
Hope is gone

I am alone
And no one knows.

Robert Wilcock (14)
Our Lady's Catholic High School

TIDAL WAVE

I could hear the waves roaring,
The rocks crashing together,
One after another,
Immense waves
Rush over the land,
Twist violently towards you.

Jessica Smith (11)
Our Lady's Catholic High School

TWIN TOWERS

Two monuments of astounding significance
Stood tall,
They towered the city.
Everything was as it should be
In the great city of the country.
No one could have predicted it,
The atrocity which was to come.
It would crumble these two
Great monuments,
What were once the central meeting point,
Of the whole world.

It was three airborne destructors,
Sent to destroy.
They did not only destroy,
They brought upset upon an unsuspecting,
Innocent, undeserving nation of good citizens.
It was a year ago when this terrible
Atrocity did happen.
It still has not been amended.

Michael McKenna (14)
Our Lady's Catholic High School

SUNSHINE

The sand is glowing like a lantern,
The sea is as still as a heavy rock,
The sun is burning us as hot as an oven,
The children are splashing all day round,
The sea is stinging our little cuts,
The adults are lazing in the sun
While we are all having fun.

Lucy Bailey (12)
Our Lady's Catholic High School

THE LONELY MAN

The lonely man
Sits alone
Reading the paper
Waiting for the phone,
Watching behind the curtain,
Waiting for the postman to arrive with bills,
Bills that brighten the lonely man's day,
Gathering the money together to pay,
Dining alone is depressing,
Especially as it's soup for one
He is desperate to have a meal with someone.
The lonely figure
That sits in the park
Feeding the ducks
Until it grows dark,
No friends to talk to
To moan to or complain
No one to play cards with
When it starts to rain,
What life is this to live alone,
Waiting for company,
Waiting for the phone.

Alison Swarbrick (14)
Our Lady's Catholic High School

THE LION

The lion runs like a swift hawk
Barely touching the ground
And to catch its prey,
Death comes to those who walk
So beware, don't stand and stare.

Robert Fazackerley (12)
Our Lady's Catholic High School

POSITIVE

Be positive,
In what you do,
Don't care
What others think.

Shout about your ideas,
Or no one will ever know,
It might be good or bad
But your idea might count.

Don't be scared
Of what you like,
Tell people when they ask
Or they may think you're boring.

If you are positive
You will go in for life,
Yes positive is the way to be,
If you are not positive
Then you will be on your own.

Christopher Morgan (14)
Our Lady's Catholic High School

THE BLAZING STORM

Clashes and bangs deafen you,
With enormous black clouds above,
Flashing lights all around you,
Animals squeaking out of fright.
You're petrified of what's going to happen,
Everybody's electric goes out,
The lightning is so strong,
So loud and so fierce.

Tasha Helm (11)
Our Lady's Catholic High School

SOMETHING!

If a person were to pick on you,
What would you do?
Could you fight back?
If no,
What about that person in the corner,
Picked on day and night.
Could you fight back for them?
Yes, you could,
But instead you do nothing,
Nothing!
Just watching, listening, yet you do nothing!
Doing nothing is just as bad as taking part.
If a person were to pick on you
If a person were to pick on someone else
What would you do?
Could you fight back?

Kim Marsden (14)
Our Lady's Catholic High School

SHARK

A large grey shadow, lurking at the bottom of the sea,
waiting patiently, for some unsuspecting fish to swim by,
like a torpedo it rockets off,
there is no chance for the fish to escape,
large, medium or small,
the big grey monster eats them all.
His feast is over, the fish have gone,
now back to the bottom of the sea it goes,
beware the big grey monster,
beware the big grey *shark!*

Catherine Purkis (12)
Our Lady's Catholic High School

TWIRLING, WHIRLING TORNADO

Tremendous, horrendous,
Whirling tornado,
Come for food.
They soon destroy,
They're growing,
Twisting, whirling,
Twister tearing
Roots off trees,
Houses off the ground,
Cows through the air,
Lamp posts whirling
With floods and floods
Of electricity
Tearing the sky
Then the tornado
Goes back to sleep.

Liam Cafferkey (11)
Our Lady's Catholic High School

TREMENDOUS TWIRLING TWISTER

Twists of wind twirling around
Houses being pulled off the ground.
In the distance you can see it,
The twirling twister coming for you,
People frightened, hiding underground,
Women, children grabbing onto each other,
Dust getting in your eyes.
It's finally over,
The twirling twister's back in the sky.

Lauren Butler-Holt (12)
Our Lady's Catholic High School

TEENAGE ROLLER COASTER

Teenage life is like a roller coaster,
You never know when you're up or down.
When you're up you're very happy,
When you're down you're very snappy.
Teenage life is like a roller coaster,
You never know when you're up or down,
When you're up you're having fun,
When you're down you're very glum.
Teenage life is like a roller coaster,
You never know when you're up or down.
When you're up you're with your mates,
When you're down you're behind the gates.
The roller coaster ends when you turn 21!

Mairead Platt (11)
Our Lady's Catholic High School

IT'S COMING

Twisting and turning,
Swishing and swirling,
Round and round and round,
It picks up people
And flattens houses.
It makes such a terrible sound
When you peer down the middle
It looks like a funnel.
Round and round and round,
People are frightened
Running for safety
In shelters underground.

Rebecca Nimmo (11)
Our Lady's Catholic High School

DIFFERENT

Stood in the corner all alone
No one knows why she's on her own
Maybe she has the wrong shoes
Or maybe no exciting news.

She stands and watches as people go by
Sometimes she just wants to die
Dreaming of one day making a friend
But the image quickly seems to end.

When people walk past calling her names
Stopping and staring at all her shames
No one knows what she's really like
Because no one cares
She's different.

Paula Riley (14)
Our Lady's Catholic High School

MY DOG

Plodding Plod, an old dog,
As slow as a snail,
But as cute as can be.
When he's naughty he looks at you,
His puppy eyes so big and brown.
He likes his food,
Eats it quick.
Woof, woof, in the night,
He's chasing cats or rabbits in his dreams,
If he sits in front of you his ears must need a scratch,
If he rolls in front of you his tummy must need a tickle,
His fur is as soft as silk,
He sleeps like a log.

Alex Bisby (12)
Our Lady's Catholic High School

SEPTEMBER 11TH

Flowers have been placed everywhere,
Littering the border, adding colour to the bareness.
Just like a bruise on a shiny, green apple,
Ground Zero lies in the midst of New York City.
The mighty Twin Towers, standing tall and proud,
Now reduced to nothingness.
Only leaving an expanse of space and tragedy.
What had an immense impact on the city's skyline,
Now a vast, desolate waste ground,
Causing such sadness and loss of loved ones.
Two important buildings with many people working,
The catastrophe arose, blotting out many lives.
People all around the world prayed and grieved,
Visitors now come to Ground Zero to pay their respects -
Being watched over by a non-existent audience.

Chloé Cooper (14)
Our Lady's Catholic High School

HOMELESS

The constant patter of people's feet,
Trying to ignore me as I sit on the street,
The strong, cold, wind biting at my face,
For homeless the streets are the wrong kind of place,
My hat for money still lies bare,
People walk past but not one of them care.
The hours pass slowly whilst on the street,
Not one kind person did I happen to meet,
The night's drawing in and it's getting dark,
I must now sleep on a bench in the park.

Katherine Moxham (15)
Our Lady's Catholic High School

THE DAY THAT SHOOK THE WORLD

The day that shook the world,
It was in the papers, on the telly - everywhere!
Friends and family destroyed
Landmarks and buildings shattered to pieces.

We held a minute's silence
Over many countries
For the ones that were lost
In this terrible tragedy,
That shook the world!

So now we'll all remember
For the rest of our lives
That tragic day, September the 11th
That shook a country, a nation
And a world!

Rachel Lonsdale (14)
Our Lady's Catholic High School

TWIN TOWERS

Two twins stood tall
each the same as each other,
no better or no worse,
but on that dreaded day
finally America's nightmare
came true.

Thousands dead
and the president said,
'We will have our revenge.'

Matt Turner (15)
Our Lady's Catholic High School

WHAT AM I?

I am an angel, angels are happy.
Happy are children, children are wonderful.
Wonderful is wicked.
Wicked is sometimes good, sometimes bad.
Sometimes good sometimes bad is chocolate.
Chocolate is my friend.
My best friend is my mum and I drive her mad.

Therefore, I am an angel, I'm a happy child.
I am wonderful, I am wicked.
I am sometimes good, sometimes bad.
I love chocolate, chocolate is my friend.
My best friend is my mum and I drive her mad.

Abi Hughes (11)
Our Lady's Catholic High School

PAPARAZZI

You must always be ready for the paparazzi,
Snap, snap, snap is all you hear,
As the camera shutter goes on and on,
The flashes are blinding but you must
Keep your stature.

The stories they make could drive you insane,
'Lies, lies, lies,' you say but no one listens.
You go insane and nobody cares,
You just become yesterday's news.

Jason Donnelly (15)
Our Lady's Catholic High School

TWISTING

Twisting and turning,
Whizzing and whirling,
Sucking like a hoover,
Sweeping anything in its path,
The sound of people screaming,
Cows mooing,
Houses twisting,
Nothing survives.

Amy Keefe (11)
Our Lady's Catholic High School

VOLCANIC FIRE

Ash darkening the sky
Lava rushing down
Incinerating all the houses
Revitalising the land,
Smells of bad eggs.

Matthew Atkinson (11)
Our Lady's Catholic High School

THE VOLCANO

The floor started to shake,
it felt like an earthquake.
Rocking and rolling.
Trees and buildings collapse,
people checking their maps.

Cracks run along the roads,
people leaving with heavy loads.
Everyone shouting,
'We have to get away from here!'

Crystal Fitch (11)
Our Lady's Catholic High School

ROBIN

It moves like the Earth.
It picks the food up with its mouth.
It bobs its head up and down.
The robin lives in a nest made of sticks.
It is a red-breasted bird
With a nice brown or grey tail and dark eyes.
It plays in a bath with its mates.

Karen Kirkham (12)
Our Lady's Catholic High School

MY DOG

My dog is a chocolate Labrador.
Not fat, not skinny, just normal.
He has big, floppy ears
like my shirt hanging out at school.
Wagging tail like a floppy flag.
Very playful like a little lad.

Adam Lee (13)
Our Lady's Catholic High School

TIME

As a child I was told
Days stretched ahead.
In truth, I thought the same -
Hours were long, holidays eternal
And tomorrow never came.

Yet as years pass
I see the lie.
Time does not stand still,
It cannot be slowed nor pushed ahead
Not bent to human will.

Always too much
Never enough,
We are told that there is plenty -
'No need to rush, do slow down,
Lots of time.' Have we?

Each day I run
To keep up with time,
Yet I always seem too slow.
I lag behind, can't get things done
And end up feeling low.

If I took the time
To stand and think
Perhaps I'd come to know
That each moment is a precious one
And when it's gone, it's gone.

Hannah Ibison (14)
Our Lady's Catholic High School